I produce and create, initiate and innovate. I live boldly, while wisely managing risks. My failures are not cause for defeat, but rather catalysts for success. I learn from each, pick myself up, and keep charging forward.

I live not for retirement, but for purpose. I develop my gifts and talents and leverage them to create value for others and fulfillment for myself.

I have one life to live, and I intend to live it fully. I live with adventure and suck the marrow out of life. I dare to dream and live with passion.

I refuse to spend my life doing the bidding of others. I will help others build their dreams but not at the expense of my own.

I build my 5 Day Weekend. I live the life I love.

EEKEND

*"Freedom begins
between the ears."*

—EDWARD ABBEY

BRIEF CONTENTS

WELCOME

WELCOME

You can change the way you live and work. You can enjoy a life rich with money, personal freedom, and purpose. The 5 Day Weekend mindset and strategies can empower you to create your own lifestyle.

As a teenager living in Melbourne, Australia, I started giving guitar lessons. It soon became a successful part-time business. I recruited a small group of instructors who worked for me. By the time I graduated from high school I was ready to takeoff to Hollywood and pursue my dream of becoming a rock star. I formed a rock band and went on tour.

I had a strong desire to create an income stream beyond the band. I worked hard and saved diligently to build cash flow from real estate and other investments. It took me eight years to have enough outside income to walk away from the band and live my 5 Day Weekend.

Your journey will be different. You may reach your goal sooner. Or, it may take you longer. It will require lots of study, hard work, and grit. If you choose to take the challenge, a life of freedom awaits you.

Extreme adventure travel and creating new global enterprises are my passion. How you live your own life of freedom is up to you. You make the choices. The 5 Day Weekend is about more and better choices.

This book shows you the big picture, the concept, the vision, a mindset and a strategy. You can tailor your 5 Day Weekend plan to fit your strengths, interests, and opportunities. My goal is to give you 1) the underlying principles you need to create and accelerate your plan, and 2) a range of possible options you can pursue.

Starter chapters help you examine an idea or strategy and decide if you want to investigate it more. To help you take the next step, there are additional free resources on the book's website.

If you're new to entrepreneurship and/or investing, you'll want to read each section in depth. Look for ideas that spark your interest, that seem viable for you, and that you want to explore. If you have entrepreneurial experience, you may be able to skim through some of my suggested opportunities and investments, while focusing on the underlying principles and philosophies that set 5 Day Weekend apart from the traditional mindset.

I've invited Garrett Gunderson to add his financial expertise. He is a *New York Times* bestselling author and the founder of an Inc. 500 firm. You will hear my voice throughout the book. Garrett will also regularly take the stage to share his expertise.

I'll give you recommendations based on my experience. But the focus is on giving you information that will help you examine how you can live a life of more freedom—to create your own vision and then begin to develop your personal plans to realize your dream.

If your primary goal in life is to get a safe and secure job with benefits, this isn't the book for you. But if you're dedicated to freedom and purpose, this book gives you the formula you've been looking for. Will you accept the 5 Day Weekend challenge?

—Nik Halik, Founder and CEO of 5 Day Weekend®

CONTENTS

PART I: THE BIG IDEA
---

3 MORE DAYS OF FREEDOM

PART II: THE FOUNDATION

KEEP MORE MONEY

PART III: INCOME GROWTH

MAKE MORE MONEY

PART IV: WEALTH CREATION

GROW MORE MONEY

PART V: THE JOURNEY

POWER UP!

PART VI: FREEDOM LIFESTYLE

LIVE YOUR PURPOSE

5 DAY WEEKEND® MANIFESTO

I own my life. I set the terms. I take responsibility for my results. I am the master of my fate, the determiner of my destiny. I live by design, not by default.

I reject the grind of 9 to 5. I escape the oppression of time clocks and bosses, commuting and cubicles.

I do not yearn for security but hunger for freedom. I renounce the dependence of jobs and benefits, and create independence through entrepreneurship.

I build businesses for cash flow, while others slave at jobs for a salary.

I create wealth by investing in assets, while others create liabilities on credit.

I am willing to do what others will not do, to get what others will not enjoy.

I hustle for a short time to fully enjoy life for a long time.

I produce and create, initiate and innovate. I live boldly, while wisely managing risks. My failures are not cause for defeat, but rather catalysts for success. I learn from each, pick myself up, and keep charging forward.

I live not for retirement, but for purpose. I develop my gifts and talents and leverage them to create value for others and fulfillment for myself.

I have one life to live, and I intend to live it fully. I live with adventure and suck the marrow out of life. I dare to dream and live with passion.

I refuse to spend my life doing the bidding of others. I will help others build their dreams but not at the expense of my own.

I build my 5 Day Weekend. I live the life I love.

EEKEND

"The minute you begin to do what you really want to do, it's really a different kind of life."

—BUCKMINSTER FULLER

Putting the 5 Day Weekend to Work

For you, this book may:

- Be a wake-up call
- Offer new ideas
- Crystalize thoughts you've had before
- Challenge you to live life to the fullest
- Spur you to action

It can be read from beginning to end to give you an overview. After finishing the book, you may decide to take the challenge. Then you can go back and use the Calls to Action, the worksheets, and the other applications throughout the book.

If, after you've read the first few chapters, you already know you want to live a free lifestyle and are ready to go to work, you can begin using the Calls to Action and other applications right away.

And you can go to our website for many resources, including downloading and printing the worksheets. You could make your own 5 Day Weekend binder, or simply create a special folder on your computer.

Keeping records and tracking your progress can help you better plan and gives you energy to move toward achieving your 5 Day Weekend.

In the book you will find this passport icon in the margin.

The icon indicates that a resource referenced in the text is on our website, 5DayWeekend.com, and is available for your use at no cost.

There's also a list of all the resources in the back of the book. To find a resource, key in the Passport Code at 5Day Weekend.com.

Somehow, we got it all wrong in our culture. It's engrained in us that we have to work a minimum of forty hours a week for at least forty years. As the plan on paper goes, we save a portion of our income and invest it for retirement. At retirement age we've accumulated a pile of cash, which we invest conservatively and then live off the interest and principal, drawing down a little each year (most pundits say 4 percent).

5 Day Weekend entrepreneurs deconstruct this mindset, turn it on its head, and see life through a completely new perspective. Instead of working hard for someone else for forty years so that you can then have a few years left over to putter away, you work hard for yourself for five to ten years so that you have the rest of your life for adventure, meaning, and joy. Instead of looking forward to a "someday" retirement, you create and live your grand purpose today.

With the 5 Day Weekend paradigm, you liberate your mind and finances. You don't invest in retirement. You eliminate retirement and choose to love life. You *never* fully retire. Instead, you retire from things you hate and embrace living a life you love.

CHAPTERS

Everyone loves weekends. Every week, we count down the days. Finally, Friday afternoon arrives and we are off the clock. We do what we have to do for five days to enjoy what we *want* to do for two. Sleep in. Take a trip with the family. Go out with friends. Attend a concert or sporting event. Enjoy a hobby. Relax with a good book.

But the whole time we are playing, Sunday evening is lurking just around the corner. All too soon, we've turned the corner and are smacked back into reality. The weekend is over. Another workweek begins. Back to the grindstone.

Once in a while a three-day weekend gives us a little more time to get away. Occasional vacations expand our opportunities. But these brief glimpses of freedom often intensify our feelings of being trapped. The time flies and they always end, forcing us to face the painful reality that we have to work hard for the majority of our lives, with no end in sight.

> "There are essentially only two drugs that Western civilization tolerates: caffeine from Monday to Friday to energize you enough to make you a productive member of society, and alcohol from Friday to Monday to keep you too stupid to figure out the prison you are living in."
>
> —BILL HICKS

Build Your Freedom Lifestyle

But what if life could be different? What if you could flip the five days on and two days off lifestyle to a five days off and two days on lifestyle? What if you could earn far more money and create far more freedom by working just two days a week and have five days to do whatever you wanted to do? And what if you could do this not just once in a while, but every week consistently for the rest of your life? What could you do with three more days of weekend every single week?

The 5 Day Weekend is both a mindset and a proven methodology for adding three more days to your weekend, every week for the rest of your life. It's a way to create a work style and lifestyle that feels like a weekend. Its outcome is more and better choices. More freedom to choose your work, personal goals, recreation, and purpose.

The 5 Day Weekend life is an unconventional way of looking at life. It's recognizing that 1) much of what we've been taught about life, finances, and earning a living has been false and misguided, and 2) the importance of cultivating a new paradigm based on a clearer version of reality. It's realizing that much of our modern paradigm is antiquated, having its roots in the Industrial Revolution —the era of assembly lines and punching time clocks. In the digital Information Age we have the freedom and opportunity to create our lives by design. We can get paid not for muscle power but for brain power.

The goal is to create enough passive income, which flows to you without a lot of ongoing effort, so that you don't have to work forty to sixty hours a week. It moves you away from work that demands you to punch a clock, report to a boss, wear a suit, keep an hourly calendar, spend hours in meetings, or dread your next performance review.

The reason so few of us are free is because we are held captive by active income. Active income is working as an employee for an hourly wage or set salary. It's billing by the hour as a self-employed professional. Or it's being self-employed and working long hours to pay the bills. If you are not physically performing the work, you don't get paid. If you stopped working right now, how long could you sustain your current lifestyle?

In the 5 Day Weekend strategy, you create passive income streams that can be managed, monitored, and grown on your schedule and your terms, with minimal time and effort. As contrasted with active income, passive income is generated on a consistent basis without requiring your constant real-time presence. It may require some ongoing management, but money still flows even when you're personally not doing the work. Money doesn't sleep. Money doesn't know about clocks, schedules, or holidays.

There are various ways to generate passive income, and in the Information Age your passive income opportunities have never been so diverse, lucrative, and sound. The aim of a 5 Day Weekend is to generate a wide range of income streams that constantly replenish your accounts and fuel your lifestyle. You control your destiny. You set your own schedule, call your own shots, and answer only to yourself.

You don't have to work long hours at your office or someone else's office. You're not bound by geography and can work where you want. You have unlimited earning possibilities. You are self-motivated, knowing there are no gatekeepers to regulate your income. Your investments work without you, often managed by a professional you have hired.

You'll never get rich by saving money. You'll only become rich by investing in assets that create cash flow and economic freedom.

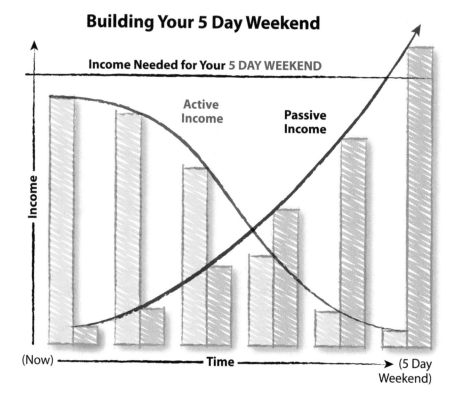

Building Your 5 Day Weekend

Income Needed for Your 5 DAY WEEKEND

Active Income

Passive Income

Income

(Now) —————————— Time —————————➤ (5 Day Weekend)

You've achieved your 5 Day Weekend goal when your passive income covers your expenses for the standard of living you want. You're able to work only fifteen to twenty hours a week instead of forty to sixty—and some weeks or months you don't have to work at all. Your freedom funds and enables your personal freedom.

What Would *Your* 5 Day Weekend Be Like?

What if you cut the amount of time you worked each week by more than half? If you added three more days to your weekend, what would you do with your time? How would you spend your 5 Day Weekend?

More of this	Less of this
Travel and getaways	Doing what you hate
Leisure time with friends	Early morning alarm
Becoming healthy and fit	Smaller paycheck
Your favorite hobby	Demanding boss
Family time	Commuting in traffic
Learning a new language	Long, boring meetings
Time just for you	Deadlines
Your spiritual life	Performance reviews
Your favorite charity	Worrying about debt
Work in your garden	Stuck and stagnant
Reading books	Suits and ties, high heels
Teaching a class	Office politics
Relaxed downtime	Feeling overwhelmed
Writing a book	Stress

What do you want less of in your life? What do you want more of? Whatever each of those answers is for you, that's what a 5 Day Weekend can give you. Imagine the possibilities. Create a vision of your personalized 5 Day Weekend. Then use this vision to fuel your drive to achieve the lifestyle you want. As you create more choices and more free time, you can spend your life in ways that provide your greatest joy,

> The ultimate quantification of success is not how much time you spend doing what you love. It's how little time you spend doing what you hate.

achieve your grandest goals, and share your abundance with your community. You are free to fully live your highest purpose. You crush the word "someday" and do the things you've always dreamed of doing today. You stop wishing and start truly living.

Most people work for their money. I'm going to show you how to get your money working for you.

"There is no small passion to be found playing small — in settling for a life that is less than the one you are capable of living."

— NELSON MANDELA

CHAPTER 2

NEW MINDSET, MORE FREEDOM

Retirement. That great American Dream. Work at a job you don't even like for forty years. Scrimp and save in retirement plans. Then become economically dead and after that, as this plan is sold to us, live the "good life."

The only problem with this plan is that *it doesn't work*. (How many people do you know who have become truly wealthy by saving in retirement plans?) Not only does it not work in practice, but the mindset is flawed. Whatever benefits may be achieved come at too high of a cost.

The primary fear of retirees is running out of money after they retire. In most cases, they seek the sanctuary and security of government social welfare programs in retirement, having contracted financial diabetes due to poor financial decision making or a broken financial system. Government programs are their shot of insulin to temporarily keep them aboveground. Others work well into their golden years just to merely survive.

The January 13, 2016, U.S. Powerball draw created the largest jackpot in world history. It had an annuity value of $1,586,400,000 and 635,103,137 total tickets were sold. Many believed that winning the lottery was the only way to become financially secure in life. The problem was the odds of winning were 1 in 292.2 million. For the sake of comparison, someone eating an oyster has better odds (1 in 12,000) of finding a pearl inside of it.

Most people work in a job on a 5:2 ratio, when they work five days and are paroled for a two-day weekend. They have no employment contract guaranteeing future employment. Sadly, they waste so much time and energy chasing a "dream job." The reality is that your real dream job does not exist. You must *create* it. You control your own destiny. You could wait until you get disrupted by your boss or the economy, or you can consciously disrupt yourself, get out of the status-quo rut, and build your 5 Day Weekend.

As a 5 Day Weekender, you reinvent yourself and break through your financial glass ceiling. You generate your own income doing what you love. You don't hand your money over to someone else to manage, where your risk is high and you have little or no control. Rather, you stay in control of your own money to reduce your risk and dramatically increase your cash flow and profitability.

> Are you doing what you love? Have you built a life you don't need a vacation from?

Instead of accumulating over long periods of time, you leverage and utilize to create exponentially greater returns. You're not working for money. You're working for the freedom of a 5 Day Weekend lifestyle.

Making these practical changes in your actions and habits requires embracing a new mindset. With a 5 Day Weekend lifestyle, you declare your entrepreneurial independence and earn your freedom. It's an entirely new outlook on life. It's a deviation from the outdated five-day workweek life that enables you to legitimately unshackle yourself and escape financial mediocrity.

Freedom vs. Security

In the conventional mindset, security, not freedom, is the overriding goal. The irony is that the security for which we sacrifice our freedom doesn't even exist, as anyone who's lost his or her job in an economic downturn can attest.

> "I am a member of a species that thinks working five days a week for forty years to pay off a debt created on a bank's computer screen is freedom."
>
> —ANONYMOUS

Most workers feel their life is put on hold. They *have* to work, which leaves them no time or financial freedom to do what they really want to do — or so they think. And most workers are dissatisfied with their jobs. As one report by the research group Conference Board showed, 52.3 percent of American workers are unhappy at work.[1] Only 46.6 percent of employees say they feel satisfied with their job security. Their dissatisfaction comes from the fact that their job doesn't allow them to enjoy the rest of their life. When you work a 9-to-5 job, you're at the mercy of your employer. They orchestrate how you spend your eight hours each day (and usually longer). They have the power to fire you anytime.

The financial model of most Americans is created by the banks and Wall Street. The average savings rate is around 4 percent. That's 4 cents out of every dollar, less than a nickel saved for every dollar earned. The average American will generate about $2 million over a lifetime. Most, if not all, of this money falls prey to the traps of consumerism. Poor people use debt to buy things that make rich people rich, whereas the rich use debt to leverage their investments into cash flow. The world's richest sixty-two people now have more wealth than the poorest 3.6 billion combined — or half the planet.

We live in an aquarium of ignorance. It's systemic and for the most part we were indoctrinated into an academic system, devoid of any financial literacy. We have been willing participants and have never challenged the status quo. Back in childhood we were taught that anything was possible, but academia constrains the limits of possibility, and academic grades define what we can or cannot do. Academia is simply a factory assembly plant for the sole purpose of producing taxpayers and providing an apprenticeship path to a job. The academic system is built to create employees, not entrepreneurs.

At what point did we lose control of ourselves? We sold ourselves into a fast food system of academic teachings, graduating with a strict No Refund Policy, not a freedom lifestyle education.

"Security is mostly a superstition. Avoiding danger is no safer in the long run than outright exposure. The fearful are caught as often as the bold ... Life is either a daring adventure or nothing."

—HELEN KELLER

We never *earn* our way to financial freedom. The only option is to raise our income-generating capability and *invest* our way to financial freedom, time freedom, and location freedom.

Job security is a myth. Taking your destiny into your own hands and learning how to become independent through your own initiative, innovation, and tenacity is ultimately the only security you have. Employees today are in a dire predicament. Job insecurity is standard protocol. Job insecurity is now officially one month's notice if you are paid monthly, and one week's notice if you are paid weekly. With developments in advanced technology, artificial intelligence, and robotics, labor markets will continue to transform. This will lead to a net loss of five million jobs in the world's leading economies by 2020, according to the World Economic Forum.[2] Nassim Nicholas Taleb wrote, "The three most harmful addictions are heroin, carbohydrates, and a monthly salary."

The Real Risk

People often say, "I could never be an entrepreneur; it's too risky." The truth is that being an employee and being controlled by market forces, your company, and your boss is far riskier. Employers are not in the business of providing guaranteed contracts of employment. Employees can only hope their employer has enough money in the bank to pay them at the end of the week. People like guarantees, but the best guarantee of a forty-hour workweek is that you'll never become financially independent. And if you do, it will be so late in life that you'll have already forfeited much of your freedom anyway.

> "The most dangerous risk of all is postponing your dreams and betting you will have the time or freedom to do it later."
> —RANDY KOMISAR

The risks of employment are becoming more and more evident as conventional retirement plans fail, inflation continues to rise, and markets become riskier as everything moves faster. The acronym VUCA, standing for volatility, uncertainty, complexity, and ambiguity, was created to describe modern times. It's only going to get worse, and the typical employee mentality simply does not prepare us to adapt and thrive in the current environment.

The goal of the 5 Day Weekend is not security, but freedom. In the security mindset, you have neither freedom nor security. But in the freedom mindset, you achieve and enjoy both. You expand your mental capacity. You participate in your own financial rescue. Don't just be a passive "librarian" of the mind, where you acquire knowledge without acting on it. You have to become a "warrior" of the mind, where you do more than learn—you also act.

Ray Bradbury wrote in *Fahrenheit 451*:

> I hate a Roman named Status Quo! Stuff your eyes with wonder, live as if you'd drop dead in ten seconds. See the world. It's more fantastic than any dream made or paid for in factories. Ask no guarantees, ask for no security, there never was such an animal. And if there

were, it would be related to the great sloth which hangs upside down in a tree all day every day, sleeping its life away. To hell with that, shake the tree and knock the great sloth down on his ass.

> People who generate over a million dollars a year never want to retire. Those who generate very little money make plans to retire.

This book is your personal invitation to shake the tree and alter the trajectory of your life forever. As someone said, "It is not the strongest of the species that survives, nor the most intelligent, but the one most responsive to change." It's the individual who raises his level of awareness, his capacity to harness new energies and investment opportunities to combat fiscal adversity, who survives and thrives. We are naturally born to evolve. Our bank balance reflects the investment in our own financial education.

The Myth of "Mailbox Money"

Before continuing, you must understand some caveats to the 5 Day Weekend. First, understand that it doesn't come easy. I'm not talking about get-rich-quick shortcuts. I'm talking about hustling like mad for a few short years, using sound and proven strategies, to provide you with unmatched freedom over the long-term.

Also, understand that the 5 Day Weekend is not some pipe dream of lazing around at the beach while checks magically show up in your mailbox forever. Remember, you'll still need to do some work. The strategies Garrett and I will show you are certainly geared more toward generating passive income. However, they still require some level of ongoing management. There are very few sources of income that are purely passive.

We'll show you how to get paid for thinking by building a team to execute for you. You will still monitor your projects and investments, but they can largely function without your physical presence and active involvement. The administration of your ideas will be outsourced to others. We'll teach you how to work smarter instead of working harder. We'll teach you a system with more efficiency and greater rewards, doing the things that create lasting wealth and a better life.

"Change your thoughts and you change your world."
—NORMAN VINCENT PEALE

"Okay," you're thinking, "the 5 Day Weekend sounds fantastic. But how do I actually do it?" Here's how:

"Rome wasn't built in a day," so the old saying goes. Well, neither will your 5 Day Weekend be built in a day. When you're building anything, there's a process to follow. It is important to see the big picture and how each part interacts with the whole. Understanding the sequential steps in the process is essential, so that you don't build something prematurely that later has to be fixed.

The 5 Day Weekend plan shifts your income sources from active to passive. It consists of the following five steps:

The Five Steps of the 5 Day Weekend Plan

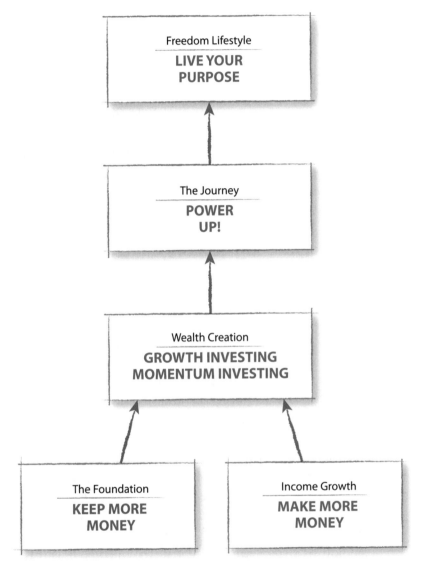

Foundation — Keep More Money

The foundation step is putting your house in order. It's looking at your existing resources and maximizing their efficiency before focusing on developing more resources. You reclaim dollars that are currently being drained from your finances using our cash flow-recovery method. This enables you to then utilize those freed-up funds for investing.

First and foremost, you have to stop the leaks in your financial bucket and keep more of what you earn. We find that more than 10 percent of most people's income is being lost to Uncle Sam, big banks, and Wall Street. Reclaiming the cash lost to these sources gives you an immediate cash flow increase without spending more time or changing any of your habits.

We use a proprietary cash flow recovery system to first find lost dollars in your income, and then to put them to better use. This system will be covered later in Part I.

Income Growth — Make More Money

The focus on this step is to increase your income as much as possible so you have cash with which to invest. Entrepreneurial income is income you earn outside of a job. Ideally, it is generated even if you're not physically present. However, it may be more active income in your early stages.

You've heard the common phrase, "It takes money to make money." This is patently untrue. Anyone can start right now with no money and create a way to make money.

However, what *is* true is that it takes money to invest. And the more you have to invest, the faster you can develop passive sources of income. Therefore, the next step is to increase your cash flow by engaging in entrepreneurial ventures. These can be done on a part-time basis, and many can be done without spending much time at all by simply leveraging your existing assets. I'll detail how to increase your entrepreneurial income in Part II.

Wealth Creation — Grow More Money

At this point, you've built a base of assets. Now the focus is on shifting your active income to passive income as quickly, safely, and efficiently as possible. You'll use your cash flow to invest in projects that will continually generate cash flow for you over time.

There are two types of investments: Growth and Momentum. Growth investments are safe, conservative, and cash-flowing. Momentum investments, on the other hand, are more speculative but offer higher upside potential. In these more aggressive investments, you remove all emotion from the equation because they are funded by your Growth investments, rather than your earned income. When successful, these investments pay out in large lump sums, and the proceeds are used to fuel more cash-flowing investments. I'll reveal more details about Growth and Momentum investments in Part II.

In the 5 Day Weekend plan, you also move away from conventional retirement plans and instead employ cash flow–optimized investments that are safer, more profitable, and that give you greater control. You create your own economy and your own stimulus plan. You move away from investments used by the middle class and instead use strategies that are normally reserved for the ultra-wealthy.

Growth Investing

In this step you start using the cash you've recovered from your existing resources and the new income you've generated to invest in more passive income streams that are conservative and safe. Save to invest, don't save to save. The only reason to save money is to invest it. This growth component is the real engine of your plan. It's your asset accumulation and cash flow–generating machine.

> When you invest, you generate money. When you spend, you purchase liabilities that will never furnish your life.

Momentum Investing

Once your new investments start generating cash flow, you have more cash to use. This allows you to chase higher-yield investments that may be speculative in nature and carry more risk. Loop and recycle any potential profits from your Momentum investments and reinvest back in Growth investments and assets.

The Journey — Power Up!

The payoff of a 5 Day Weekend is a lifestyle of freedom. But before enjoying the payoff, you must pay the price. Achieving your 5 Day Weekend requires that you conquer adversity, overcome your weaknesses, leverage your gifts, and become your best self. This is done through four key disciplines: strengthening your mindset, building your inner circle, fortifying your habits, and amplifying your energy.

When most people start out, most if not all of their income is active. To shift to more passive income streams, resources are required to invest. You start by creating as much discretionary, investable income as possible from your existing resources. Next, you start side projects to increase your income.

Once you've put enough money together, you start investing. You start by investing in yourself. If you have less than $5,000, invest in yourself by seeking mentoring, taking courses, and reading books. As your knowledge increases, you'll be surprised by the investment opportunities that arise for you.

Once you start investing, your investments build over time, thus shifting your income from active to passive. Depending on your starting point and how aggressive and effective you are with the process, within five to ten years the majority of your income should be passive, and you'll be able to work two days and enjoy five days of weekend each week.

Freedom Lifestyle — Live Your Purpose

With enough passive income streams in place, your investments can now fund and service your lifestyle and freedom. This may mean buying an expensive car or a luxurious villa overseas, or enjoying unforgettable getaways to the most exotic regions of the world. It may be spending more time with your favorite charity or underwriting an important cause.

> "Rebels are the people who refuse the seen for the unseen."
>
> —ANNE DOUGLAS SEDGWICK

CHAPTER 4

The key to achieving your freedom lifestyle is transforming your income from active to passive. As you work through the five steps in the 5 Day Weekend plan, you initially will add more active income through entrepreneurial enterprises. Next, you will structure your businesses so that they require less of your time. And you will build assets that can become more and more passive—investments that will produce cash flow without your active involvement.

The Active/Passive Income Scale

The Active/Passive Scale shows ways that income can be earned. It profiles various types of work according to the degree they are active or passive. However, it is not precise. Between the most active and the most passive, there is a range of ways to earn income that involves the nature of the work, how often you have to perform it, and whether or not your presence is required.

The source of most people's income is active. That's the most common way to acquire income. On the other end of the scale, there are fewer ways that are increasingly more passive.

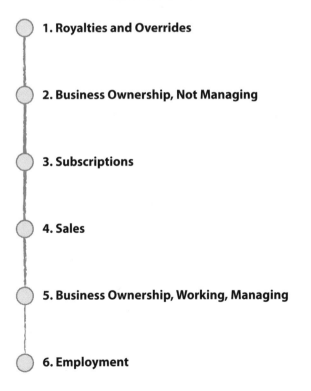

The Active/Passive Scale

MOST PASSIVE

1. Royalties and Overrides

2. Business Ownership, Not Managing

3. Subscriptions

4. Sales

5. Business Ownership, Working, Managing

6. Employment

MOST ACTIVE

MOST PASSIVE TO MOST ACTIVE INCOME

○ 1. Income from Royalties and Overrides

- Intellectual property such as patents, copyrights (books, song lyrics, music, etc.), trademarks, and URLs. You hold legal claim and can license, lease, or transfer for an on-going royalty or fee.
- Mineral rights such as oil, gas, or water. You hold legal claim and can license, lease, or transfer for an ongoing royalty or fee.
- Overrides or commissions on the sale of products or services. This can be income from your own work or from work by others made within your organization, such as direct marketing company overrides and insurance commissions. After the sale, there may be little or no ongoing work.
- Property leases or rentals. Ongoing income from land or building agreements. Farm or ranch land leases may provide income with little or no work from the owner. Rental property typically requires some involvement by the owner—warehouses or storage units require less, residential housing more.
- Earning Bitcoin or any other cryptocurrency with shares in a mining pool.

Frequency of Work: Monitor and maintain. After an agreement is executed there can be an ongoing stream of income. Then the owner has to do little work.

Physical Presence: Rarely required.

○ 2. Owning a Business but Not Managing It

Net income from a business that you own fully or partially, but that is managed by someone else. Income may be monthly, quarterly, yearly, or whenever profit is produced.

Frequency of Work: Quarterly or regular meetings with management, examination of financial statements, and preparation of taxes is typically required, and there may be additional onsite visits from time to time.

| **Physical Presence:** Rarely required.

⚪ **3. Subscriptions**

Recurring income for membership or service agreements.

Frequency of Work: Periodic, depending on needed updates or new services.

Physical Presence: Infrequent, often automated.

⚪ **4. Sales**

Income directly from commissions from the sale of goods or services. Real estate, insurance, direct marketing, and a wide variety of other types of sales, including technology, pharmaceuticals, and business services. Income is a percentage of the sales amount or a flat fee. You may be an independent contractor or an employee.

Frequency of Work: Varies greatly depending on whether you're an independent contractor or an employee.

Presence: Not required on an ongoing basis. Focus is on performance, not presence.

⚪ **5. Owning a Business, Working in It, Managing It**

Salary and/or income from the profits of a business that you own fully or partially. Your participation in the business is significant and often requires long hours.

Frequency of Work: Typically 40 hours a week, often more.

Presence: Often onsite or with daily operations.

⚪ **6. Employment**

Income paid for work done by the hour, day, week, month, project, or job. Compensation may be an annual salary, project or job fee, or piece rate. You are paid only for work produced or services rendered, or clocked time.

Frequency of Work: Five days a week and possible work on weekends for a full-time job. For part-time work, usually every week.

Presence: Usually onsite. If offsite, there are typically reporting requirements regarding documentation of work done.

Develop Your Passive Income Ratio

I use the term "Active Income Ratio" (AIR) to describe the ratio of people's earned income to their expenses. Most people start out each month with a 0:1 ratio, meaning that they have nothing with which to cover their monthly expenses until they earn money actively from a job. The objective is to get to a 1:1 ratio at the end of the month (enough money coming in to equal their expenses). In some cases, people don't even reach that ratio and fall back on credit cards to make up the difference. Some even use cash advances on their credit cards as a Ponzi scheme to service the interest payments on other credit cards. Credit cards are now perceived as supplemental income. At a 1:1 ratio, 100 percent of your earning activities are spent trading time for money and servicing lifestyle and liabilities.

What you want to develop instead is a Passive Income Ratio (PIR), referring to the amount of passive income generated in relation to your expenses. A 1:1 PIR means that you're generating enough passive income to cover your monthly expenses. This is where you hit the fast track, because every dollar you earn actively isn't required to live or provide for your lifestyle. Therefore, you can invest earned dollars to build cash-flowing assets. This is where you gain a distinct advantage.

Your minimum goal is to get to a 2:1 ratio, generating twice the amount of passive income as you need to cover your monthly expenses. A 2:1 ratio provides a contingency of surplus funds. This is what I call "seatbelt investing." So if your current monthly expenses are $5,000, you want to develop passive income streams that generate $10,000 per month (plus you'll still probably have active income from either a job or your entrepreneurial activity, or both). Think of how much anxiety and stress you can alleviate by developing a 2:1 PIR ratio.

I achieved my 2:1 Passive Income Ratio when I was performing in a rock band. While still collecting money from royalties, merchandise, and touring revenue, I was also generating more than $22,000 per month from residential real estate with a portfolio of about seventeen properties at the time. I left the music industry after achieving my 2:1 PIR.

Passive Income Ratio

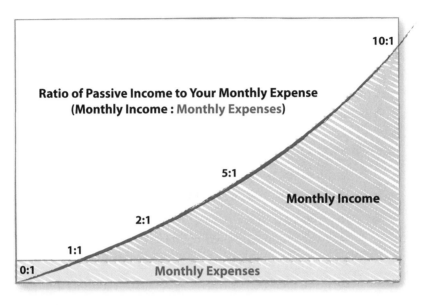

A 2:1 ratio gives you your exit strategy to leave your job. You don't necessarily have to leave, but you at least have the option if you want. Or, you can keep the job and start investing 100 percent of your active income into passive income investments to continue scaling up your PIR.

"Rich people choose to get paid based on results. Poor people choose to get paid based on time."
—T. HARV EKER

Once you're at a 2:1 ratio, you keep growing that to hit a progressively higher ratio. My definition of financial independence is having a 5:1 PIR, and I define sustainable financial wealth as having a 10:1 PIR. Assuming monthly expenses of $5,000, a 5:1 PIR equals $25,000 and a 10:1 PIR equals $50,000 in monthly passive income.

Passive Income Score Sheet

This score sheet helps you determine how active or passive any business venture or investment is.

Analyze the passive potential of any opportunity or investment by rating the following factors. Rate each one on a scale of 1 through 5; 1 = low potential and 5 = high potential.

Investment name _____

☐ **1. Immediate cash flow**
   Will there be income soon (5), or will it take longer (1)?

☐ **2. Regular cash flow**
   Will the income be predictable (5) or sporadic (1)?

☐ **3. Sustainable cash flow**
   Will the income continue (5) or last for a limited time (1)?

☐ **4. Increasing cash flow**
   Can the income increase over time? Yes (5). No (1).

☐ **5. Your personal time to manage**
   Hours per month of your time? None (5). A lot (1).

☐ **6. Onsite management**
   Do you need to be present? None (5). A lot (1).

☐ **Total score for this investment**

Anything with a score lower than 10 should be either restructured to increase the passive cash flow or eliminated. Anything between 10 and 20 should be modified to maximize the passive potential. Anything above 25 is a great passive investment.

Go to 5DayWeekend.com to use this interactive score sheet to calculate your scores, or you can download and print for your use.
Code: P1

The Active Income Trap

Enhanced lifestyle is, of course, the aim and benefit of increasing income. The entire 5 Day Weekend process is designed to give you the lifestyle of your dreams. However, keep in mind that lifestyle is the last step in the process. People stay stuck and get into big trouble when they increase their monthly expenses and take shortcuts on the path to a bigger, better lifestyle. These shortcuts take one of two forms:

> **"Shortcuts make long delays."**
> —J. R. R. TOLKIEN

Using Active Income to Fund Lifestyle

The first reason people stay stuck in the trap of active income is that they go straight from income to lifestyle. First of all, they have just one source of income—a job—which alone is a great risk. Then, instead of investing as much of their income as possible for their future benefit, they use their income to fund their lifestyle. They have no goose that produces gold without their effort, and whatever gold they earn through personal effort is spent on depreciating liabilities, such as cars, furniture, and expensive vacations.

> Create a goose that lays golden eggs first and you'll never run out of gold.

Leveraging the 5 Day Weekend process to your advantage requires first and foremost the ability to manage and defer lifestyle. As Brian Tracy says, "The ability to discipline yourself to delay gratification in the short term in order to enjoy greater rewards in the long term is the indispensable prerequisite for success."

Avoid the trap of instant gratification and the desire to accumulate liabilities. The goal is to create a solid foundation of assets, and then the cash flow generated by your assets can be used to fund your lifestyle. The way to achieve your 5 Day Weekend lifestyle is to use your active income to fund basic living expenses, with the remaining going toward passive income–generating assets. Create a goose.

Using Active Income on Momentum Investments

People get into trouble when they skip from the income phase to the momentum phase without knowing what they're doing. In other words, they speculate and gamble on big, high-risk projects without understanding the fundamentals of investing. They hope and pray for a big payout, having little or no control over the investment. They want big money fast.

> There is no shortage of money on this planet, only a shortage of people thinking big enough.

Almost always, what happens in this scenario is they lose everything they've invested. And even when it works, they typically end up losing it all anyway because, by taking a shortcut, they haven't developed the necessary skills and discipline to keep it.

You'll learn more about the various types of strategies for Growth and Momentum investments later. For now, it's critical to understand that the order of the process matters a great deal. Each step builds on the preceding step. As in all areas of life, shortcuts in finances create nothing but long-term heartache.

You've Never Had Greater Opportunity

The 5 Day Weekend is not a strategy reserved exclusively for the smart, clever, talented, connected, formally educated, or wealthy. It's a strategy that *anyone* can apply.

> "You miss 100% of the shots you don't take."
>
> —WAYNE GRETZKY

Don't let yourself make excuses. Don't think, "Well, some people may be able to do this, but it won't work for me." You can do this. You have opportunities available to you that your ancestors could never have dreamed of.

If your life isn't working, the problem isn't your life — it's you. Don't waste your life making excuses and following the herd. Don't follow parked cars and sit around waiting for opportunity — get off the couch and go create opportunity. Don't wait for your ship to come in — go build it.

Freedom can be yours. The time is now.

"If you don't find a way to make money while you sleep, you will work until you die."

—WARREN BUFFETT

Call to Action

Your 5 Day Weekend Plan

Create your personal 5 Day Weekend vision.

Your Vision

What would your 5 Day Weekend look like? How would you spend your time? What would you do less of and do more of?

Your Earnings and Expenses

How much net active money are you earning?
How much are your monthly minimum expenses?
How much net passive money are you earning?

Your Goals

When do you want to achieve your 1:1 Passive Income Ratio (earning enough passive income to cover your monthly expenses)?
Target date?

What is your goal for achieving a 2:1 Passive Income Ratio (earning twice as much passive income to cover your expenses)?
Target date?

What is your goal for achieving financial independence with a 5:1 Passive Income Ratio?
Target date?

What is your goal for achieving sustainable financial wealth with a 10:1 Passive Income Ratio?
Target date?

Go to our website to download and print this worksheet at 5DayWeekend.com.
Code: P2

"If you see it in your mind, you will hold it in your hand."
—BOB PROCTOR

Is being rich only about earning more money? Have you ever met someone who makes more money than you, yet always seems to be under financial duress?

Before engaging in the time, risk, or effort of earning more, the best place to start is to maximize the efficiency of your existing resources—to recapture dollars that are currently being lost to inefficiencies. You may discover, as most people do, that you actually have a lot more to work with than you think.

The 5 Day Weekend plan is a logical, sequential process. For it to work properly, each step must be completed at the right time, in the right way. When you take steps out of order, the result is inefficiency at the least and disaster at the worst. You must get your financial house in order first.

CHAPTERS

- **Crush Your Debt**

- **Manage Your Expenses**

- **Plug Cash Flow Leaks**

- **Capture Wealth**

- **The Rockefeller Formula**

- **Rock-Solid Financial Baseline**

- *Call to Action*

Your Debt Free Plan

CHAPTER 5

Debt. That great financial enemy we'd all love to defeat, that crushing burden we're all trying to relieve. Most of us hate it, yet nearly everyone has it. People get in it, and are trying to get out of it.

People struggle to get out of debt for two primary reasons. First, they don't have a wise and coherent strategy for paying debt down. Many competing strategies exist, but people aren't sure which one is the most effective. Second, no strategy addresses the underlying psychological reasons why people get into debt in the first place. And without addressing these reasons, they can never develop the discipline to get out and stay out of debt.

Sometimes the only way to get out of a hole is to stop digging. Financial pain may be inevitable for the ignorant. Financial suffering is optional if you choose to raise your financial IQ. Avoid debt that doesn't pay you. Make it a rule that you never use debt that won't make you money.

On the technical side, we'll give you a four-step strategy for paying down your debt. As for the discipline, you'll have to develop that on your own as you become self-aware of why you're getting into debt.

As you face and crush your debt burden once and for all, you can then turn your focus to increasing your production and cash flow.

The Best Way to Pay Off Loans

Remember that your purpose in paying off debt is to free up cash flow that you can then use to invest in passive income vehicles. With that in mind, here's the fastest, safest, and most sustainable way to become debt-free:

1. Build Savings First

It doesn't make any sense to start making higher payments to reduce your debt before you have at least three months of income, and ideally six months, in a liquid savings account. This creates safety.

If you have no cash reserves, what happens when you pay down your loans but then experience an unexpected cash flow crunch? You simply increase your loan balances again or, even worse, miss payments and hurt your credit score, therefore getting charged more for future loans.

2. Restructure Your Loans

You can restructure your loans by rolling short-term, high-interest loans into long-term, low-interest, tax-deductible loans. The goal here is to minimize your payments and maximize your cash flow.

For example, if you have enough home equity, you can refinance your mortgage, which can be a tax-deductible loan, and roll as many of your non-deductible loans (credit cards, auto, etc.) into it as possible. This will typically lower your minimum monthly loan payments, and the tax deduction will also increase your cash flow. Then you can attack your remaining loans strategically, using your increased cash flow to eliminate one loan at a time.

3. Attack One Loan at a Time

After minimizing your payments and maximizing your cash flow, you're now prepared to focus on one loan at a time until you're completely debt-free.

Most financial advisors and pundits will tell you to pay off your loans with the highest interest rates first. My advice is to ignore the interest rate and use a technique developed by Garrett and his team called the Cash Flow Index, which helps you determine which loan to pay off first.

To determine your Cash Flow Index for each loan, divide the loan balance by the minimum monthly payment. A low Cash Flow Index means the loan is inefficient. A loan with a high Cash Flow Index is efficient. As you can see on the chart below, any loan with a Cash Flow Index between 0 and 50 is in the danger zone and should be restructured or eliminated as quickly as possible. Any loan with a Cash Flow Index greater than 100 is in the freedom zone and is not a priority to pay off.

Cash Flow Index

Cash Flow Index = Loan Balance ÷ Minimum Monthly Payment

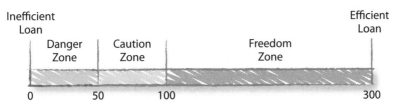

The loan to pay off first is the one with the lowest Cash Flow Index. For example, consider the following loans and ask yourself which one you would pay off first:

Loan	Balance	Interest Rate	Minimum Monthly Payment	Cash Flow Index
Mortgage	$228,000	7%	$1,665	137 ($228,000 ÷ $1,665)
Auto	$16,500	8%	$450	37 ($16,500 ÷ $450)
Credit Card	$13,000	12%	$260	50 ($13,000 ÷ $260)

In this example, it seems to make sense to pay off the credit card first because it has the highest interest rate. But the Cash Flow Index reveals that the auto loan should be paid off first. By doing so, you free up more monthly cash, which can then be applied toward the credit card balance. And then you can pay off both loans faster than if you started with the credit card.

The trick is to pay off the loan that gives you the greatest cash flow with the least investment.

4. Be Cautious About Locking Money in an Asset

Paying extra money to your mortgage can sometimes make sense when you're financially stable, but other times it's just locking money into hard-to-access equity. This strategy isn't just about paying off debt faster and saving money on interest. It's also about reducing your risk.

A good rule here is to only put extra money into debt where your minimum payment goes down as your balance goes down, such as with a credit card. Otherwise, you're worsening your Cash Flow Index with every payment. It doesn't give you immediate benefit, and it increases your risk by reducing your liquidity.

A better move is to save the money that you would have paid on the loan balance in a separate account. Then let it accumulate and earn interest until you have enough to pay off the loan in full. (For more details on this, see chapters 8 and 9 for the strategy for creating and capturing wealth.)

Why You're in Debt

Without a fundamental change in consciousness regarding debt, none of these strategies will work long-term. For lasting results, identify and solve the root causes of debt, rather than hacking at the by-products (interest and bondage).

Before you employ the techniques above, ask yourself:

- Why did I incur each of my debts? What was the purpose?
- Was my desire to consume or to produce?
- Could I have waited six months? A year?
- When I've incurred debt, how did I justify it?
- Do I seek consolation in material things?
- Was my debt caused by investments I made that were actually more like gambling—putting money into things I didn't understand and couldn't control? If so, what can I learn from this and how can I be wiser in the future?
- Was the debt due to a lack of preparation? Or a financial surprise from which I can protect myself in the future?

Getting and staying out of debt requires a fundamental shift. A simple guide moving forward: *Never borrow to consume.* Use cash for consumer items, such as furniture, clothing, and vacations, and only borrow for productive assets and resources.

> If you're born poor, it's not your mistake. But if you die poor, it is your mistake.

Getting your financial house in order is about much more than the technicalities of finance. It's about your mindset and psychology. It's about your willpower to defer immediate gratification in favor of long-term freedom. It's about seeing and cultivating a vision beyond working 9 to 5 for the rest of your life. You extend your runway in life and expand your bandwidth.

As you crush your debt, you will free up more cash flow that can be used to fund your investments.

> "Today I will do what others won't, so tomorrow I can accomplish what others can't."
>
> —JERRY RICE

CHAPTER 6

MANAGE YOUR EXPENSES

A t this point I want to backtrack a bit to provide some context and nuance on debt.

Debt vs. Liabilities

Debt is usually defined as any borrowed money. But defined
more technically, debt is having liabilities that are greater than
our assets. Liabilities are expenses that we have to pay for, such as
a mortgage, car loans, or credit cards. Assets, such as land, buildings, businesses, precious metals, and intellectual property rights,
result in cash flow or can be converted into cash flow. The market
value of your home is an asset; your mortgage is a liability.

Debt vs. Liabilities

	Market Value	Liability Amount Owed	Assets Equity	Debt
House 1	$250,000	$200,000	$50,000	$0
House 2	$250,000	$260,000	$0	$10,000

Suppose your home is worth $250,000 and you owe $200,000 on your mortgage. Traditionally, we would say you are $200,000 in debt. More technically from an accounting standpoint, you have $50,000 in equity, which is the opposite of debt. On the other hand, if you were to owe $260,000 on a home worth $250,000, you would have $10,000 of debt.

This may sound like I'm splitting hairs, but it's critical to understand the difference between debt and liability. If your goal is to stop all forms of borrowing, then you eliminate the possibility of borrowing for productive use, such as investing or business growth.

To get out of debt doesn't necessarily mean to pay off all loans. Rather, it means being in a position where your assets always exceed your liabilities. Your balance sheet, which itemizes your assets and liabilities, determines whether you have an overall equity position or an overall debt position.

5 Day Weekenders analyze loans, liabilities, and assets from a different, more sophisticated and technical standpoint than is typically taught by most pundits. Our goal isn't to simply pay off all loans. Rather, it is to maximize the efficiency and production of our cash flow. In this context, we may be okay with certain loans or have a different loan payoff priority than others might recommend. You might, in fact, choose to *increase* your liabilities in order to increase your production—all while staying technically out of debt.

To make this more concrete, when I show you how to crush your debt, I'm mostly referring to consumer debt, such as credit cards used to purchase depreciating liabilities such as clothes, furniture, and toys. This destructive type of debt is nothing but a drain on your finances. It may add to your immediate lifestyle, but at the expense of your long-term freedom.

For further clarification, let's explore different types of expenses, as categorized by Garrett.

Just One Expense to Cut

We're taught to believe that expenses are bad and to cut them as much as possible, but that perspective is simplistic and misguided. In reality, there are four types of expenses, and only one of them needs to be cut.

1. Lifestyle (Consumptive) Expenses

These are things such as dining out, vacations, concert tickets, and flat-screen TVs. These are expenses that are fun and build memories, but that don't build assets or income. You can spend money on things you value guilt-free if you make sure not to spend more than you earn or don't go into debt.

That said, it's important not to cut all these expenses out. People are taught to wait until retirement to spend any of their hard-earned money, and that only in retirement can they really enjoy life. That's why there are so many miserable millionaires! If you never spend any money, you won't be fulfilled; you won't have many enjoyable experiences. These are good expenses, as long as they are managed wisely.

Garrett teaches people to analyze lifestyle expenses on the basis of price, opportunity cost, and value to determine if a purchase is worth it.

- Price: What you pay to purchase something
- Opportunity Cost: The benefit you could have received, but forfeited, to take another course of action
- Value: The total value, real and perceived, derived from a purchase

Consider purchases within the context of your 5 Day Weekend lifestyle to decide if you'd rather sacrifice or enjoy something now. To pay for these expenses, never borrow and always use cash. Ideally, you should use the recurring revenues from your investment portfolio to pay for these.

In short, lifestyle expenses should be managed wisely.

2. Protective Expenses

These are things that protect your property and human life value. This is the financial area that most often gets overlooked—especially by the middle class. Affluent people almost always take care of this and don't compromise with their protection. They understand that there are unexpected financial surprises and issues that put their assets at risk.

Protective expenses include your liquid savings, which should be enough to cover a minimum of six months' expenses. These savings won't be overly productive in terms of earning interest, but they will be there to protect you and prevent you from worrying about money every second. Other protective expenses include estate planning, corporate structure planning, life insurance, disability insurance, medical insurance, auto insurance, and emergency preparedness.

3. Productive Expenses

Productive expenses allow you to build assets, expand your cash flow, and grow your business. This could include purchasing a tax lien or rental property. If you own a business, it might be hiring a great employee. It could be an expense such as education, whereby new opportunities are opened for you.

These are expenses that if you put a dollar into them, more than a dollar comes out the other side, like any asset that creates cash flow and appreciates in value. These are expenses that are going to enhance your life now *and* in the future—not something that will dissipate, like a consumptive expense. They may have a liability attached to them, such as a mortgage on a rental property, but by incurring them you're in a better overall position. These types of expenses should be increased and enhanced as much as possible.

4. Destructive Expenses

Destructive expenses include consumer debt, overdraft fees, and unnecessary expenses, such as a gym membership you don't use or loans that lead to debt. In a general sense, these are expenses that take value away from your life instead of adding to it. This also includes expenses for vices and weaknesses such as harmful drugs and gambling. These are the expenses that should be cut and eventually eliminated altogether.

When you understand the difference between true debt and mere liabilities, you begin to see that in many instances the way to become wealthier is to increase, not decrease, your liabilities. The cost of purchasing a tax lien, for example, is a liability. But it comes with an asset that can make you more money than it costs. If you think all liabilities are the enemy, then you'll never understand how you can safely and wisely borrow to produce.

Remember: Your goal isn't simply to "get out of debt." That's just one piece of a much bigger puzzle. Your goal is financial independence and the 5 Day Weekend.

> "Wealth, like a tree, grows from a tiny seed."
> —GEORGE S. CLASON

CHAPTER 7

PLUG CASH FLOW LEAKS

Imagine you're trying to fill a leaky bucket with water. You put a hose in it and turn the water on. As the water rises, it starts gushing out of holes in the bucket. What would be a smarter way to fill the bucket: Increase the flow so that the water coming in is greater than the water going out, or stop and plug the holes in the bucket first?

The answer is obvious. Unfortunately, it's not so obvious when it comes to finances. Everyone who hasn't achieved financial independence thinks they're not rich because they don't make enough money. They have to make more money, so the logic goes, so that they can then have discretionary income to invest. In other words, they try to turn up the water flow while ignoring the holes in their bucket. Furthermore, most people don't even see the leaks.

Most personal finance gurus will tell you that the key is cutting your expenses and scrimping like a miser. But there's a much smarter way. You can free up substantial amounts of monthly cash flow without tightening your belt and budget. The best places to look aren't your daily latte or your cable budget. Rather, they are places like your insurance and taxes, which can yield far more cash flow if structured more efficiently.

Some people really do need to reel in their expenditures. They're spending freely with no regard to the future. They're addicted to consuming. I'm not saying you shouldn't give any consideration at all to your consumptive expenses. I'm simply saying you can't shrink your way to wealth—you have to work smart, not just hard.

In Garrett's experience in working with thousands of people, more than 10 percent of most people's income is being lost in ways they don't even see, such as overpaying on taxes and paying for hidden investment fees. When you discover and plug these holes in your bucket, your income is immediately increased without changing any of your spending habits. Sacrificing a bit may help expedite the process, but some of the ways in which you can recover the most cash flow follow.

Boost Your Credit Score

Your credit score can be leveraged to your advantage. **A maximized credit score (ideally 780 or higher) is the key** to restructuring loans to free up cash flow, getting lower interest rates, paying less on insurance, and more. If you can boost your credit score, you can often negotiate better interest rates, or transfer a balance to a loan with a lower interest rate. To get your most accurate credit scores that are used by creditors, go to myFICO.com.

Aside from paying your bills on time, here are the three most important things you can do to boost your credit score:

1. **Fix errors on your credit reports.** According to a congressionally mandated study by the U.S. Federal Trade

Commission, one out of every five consumers has an error on at least one of their three credit reports.[3] An error on your credit report can make the difference between being approved or denied for a loan or getting a high or low interest rate.

The credit reporting agencies are required by law to give you a free look at your credit report once a year at Annual CreditReport.com. One strategy I recommend is to request one free report from one bureau every four months. That way you can regularly monitor your credit and check for errors for free. However, if you haven't checked any of your credit reports in years, pay the extra money to check them all for errors now, and go the free route moving forward.

Check your report regularly for misreported limits, duplicate accounts, and anything else that's incorrect. If you do find errors, don't dispute more than three errors at a time with the same bureau.

2. **Manage credit cards wisely.** It's best to have three to five credit cards with the maximum limit that you can qualify for. Don't get as many as you can. If you're applying for credit cards more than three or four times a year, you're going to have a five to fifteen point decrease in your score. The ideal amount of inquiries in a period of two years is two. Keep your balance low at all times — no higher than 30 percent of your limit, but the lower the better. And don't cancel old cards. The length of the card's credit history helps your score.

3. **Have an installment loan within the last two years of your credit history.** This is a loan for a fixed period of time with a fixed minimum payment, such as a car loan or lease, a jewelry loan, or a signature loan.

Restructure Your Loans

One of the first places to look where you're losing money is your loans. If you haven't renegotiated your interest rates or restructured your loans in the last two years or so, you're probably overpaying interest or potentially harming your cash flow.

Here are a few strategies that may be helpful, depending on your unique situation:

- Roll high-interest, non-deductible loans into low-interest, tax-deductible loans. For example, you could refinance your home and roll your credit cards into your new mortgage.
- Refinance your mortgage.
- If your car is paid off, you may want to refinance it and use the loan to pay off a higher interest rate loan.
- Use a loan from a cash value insurance policy to pay off a higher interest rate loan.
- Lengthen the term on the loan to lower the payment and improve the Cash Flow Index.
- Get a loan from a retirement plan to pay off a high interest-rate loan.
- Get a loan from a family member or friend using a promissory note. Pay them more interest than the bank gives them but less than the bank is charging you.

Real Life Stories

Jordan Cooper is a dentist who started working with Garrett to free up cash, streamline his finances, and grow his business. The first thing they did was look at his loans—a total of sixteen that needed work. They identified the worst loans, which had either short terms or high interest. They refinanced about half of his debt, which helped recapture almost $20,000 a month in cash flow. Jordan is now investing this increased cash flow back into his business.

Ben and Joyce Frank own a youth ice hockey club with three locations in Southern California. They learned the benefits of restructuring loans at an event with Garrett. While on a break at the event, Ben called two companies they had loans with and asked about the possibility of restructuring their payments. Since they had made all their payments on time, both companies agreed. They extended the length of the loan and lowered the monthly payment, which saved them $1,500 a month on one loan and $1,000 a month on the other.

Ben said, "We'd really bootstrapped our business for the first five years, so increasing our monthly cash flow was a big deal. With that cash flow, we've been able to hire more and better people, which then allows us to focus more on working on the business. We've also improved our technology and systems. When you free up a few thousand dollars a month of cash flow, it has ripple effects because now it frees up our time to focus on the next bigger thing and everything just accelerates."

Structure Your Insurance Properly

Poorly structured insurance is another common area where most people are leaking cash. Here are a few areas to consider:

1. **Raise your deductibles.** The lower your deductible, the higher your monthly premium. The reason you have insurance is for major losses, so it usually doesn't make sense to have a low deductible. If your deductible is low and you make a claim, your premiums will rise. I recommend raising your deductibles to $1,000 or even to $2,500, depending on the company and how much savings it provides.
2. **Check for duplicate or unnecessary coverage.** You may have too many policies that cover the same thing. One example would be an umbrella policy that has more than the required minimums on car and homeowner's liability for the umbrella to kick in. Consider dropping policies that do not cover the catastrophic events: short-term disability policies, accidental death and dismemberment, and other policies with limited coverage.
3. **Use umbrella policies to coordinate insurance.** Umbrella policies provide liability coverage over and above your automobile or homeowner's policy. So if your liability coverage isn't enough to cover damages, a personal umbrella insurance policy kicks in when your other liability underlying limits have been reached. An umbrella policy can protect you when your automobile or homeowner's insurance isn't enough. With properly structured umbrella

policies you can often double your coverage while lowering your premiums.

4. **Use a health savings account.** A health savings account (HSA) is a tax-advantaged medical savings account available to U.S. citizens who are enrolled in a high-deductible health plan (HDHP). The funds contributed to an account are not subject to federal income tax at the time of deposit. (Because health insurance laws are subject to change, be sure to check current policies regarding HSAs.)

5. **Extend elimination period on disability insurance.** The elimination period is the period of time between the onset of a disability and the time you are eligible for benefits. It's essentially the deductible period for disability insurance. Premiums are extremely high for 30- or 60-day periods. Premiums drop substantially for 180-day periods or longer.

6. **Combine long-term care insurance with life insurance.** Long-term care insurance may be unnecessary if you have a proper provision on your life insurance death benefit (an accelerated death benefit rider).

Incorporate for Tax Advantages

If you haven't set up a legal entity, such as an LLC or S Corp, you're overpaying in taxes. Business owners get tons of tax breaks that employees don't. In fact, there are 5,900 pages in the tax code and, of those, roughly 300 are for W2 and 1099 employees. The other 5,600 pages are ways you can get tax deductions through business ownership.

It doesn't matter if you have employees or an office. In the 5 Day Weekend lifestyle you are going to have some form of a business. Set up an entity as quickly as possible, and coordinate with a CPA to take advantage of the following possible deductions and many, many more.

*   **Home Office Deduction:** Do you make phone calls or use a computer? Make a room in your home a dedicated workspace for your business and deduct it as a home office expense.

- **Phone, Internet, and Utilities:** You can deduct the phone, fax, and internet expenses associated with your business, as well as a percentage of utilities.
- **Meals and Entertainment:** When you're traveling for business or meeting with a client, you can deduct your meals. Certain entertainment expenses are also deductible.
- **Car:** Any time you drive for business purposes you can deduct your expenses.
- **Travel:** Travel for business purposes is tax deductible.
- **Education:** Education costs related to maintaining or improving your skills for your business are tax deductible.
- **Hire Your Kids:** IRS rules allow you to pay your kids for specific tasks and deduct what you pay them.
- **Use of Your Home:** You can rent your home to your business for fourteen days or less to host functions for employees or vendors, and take the tax deduction for the business without claiming it as personal income.

Obviously, the tax code is more complex than these simple descriptions, and you'll want to use a qualified CPA to take advantage of all deductions and to stay within the rules.

Which type of entity you need depends on a variety of factors, including tax benefits, liability protection, business succession and exit strategies, and future financing and investment criteria, just to name a few. For those that need a simple structure and flexibility in a partnership, an LLC can be effective. For other, more sophisticated businesses, the need to structure a business based on tax planning can be of primary importance. Consult with an attorney to choose the right entity for your purposes and needs.

CPAs Maximize Tax Deductions

If you already have an entity established, you can probably still save money in taxes. In fact, in Garrett's work with thousands of entrepreneurs, more than 93 percent of them have been found to be overpaying taxes by not taking advantage of the right rules.

For example, many business owners can cut their current tax bill in half with one simple fix. Business owners put in a lot of time working *in* their business, such as working with clients, treating patients, or dealing with customers. The government considers money made from these activities to be "earned income," which is taxed at your normal tax rate. Currently, if you take home more than $117,000 a year in the U.S., the IRS takes 39.5 percent of every dollar you make over that amount. And beyond that, there's potentially a 15.3 percent self-employment tax if you aren't differentiating your income and set up with the right corporate structure.

One little-known provision in the tax code lets you legally pay 15.3 percent less on your income. The IRS treats investment income (such as stock dividends or rental income) differently. Unlike earned income, this money is not taxed at the additional 15.3 percent. It's actually the perfect strategy for small business owners that big businesses don't get to use. The IRS considers the time you spend working *on* your business an investment. So they tax any money you make during that time as a dividend. This can make a huge difference to your bottom-line profits.

There are certain rules about this, and you need to make sure you do it right. And this is just one of at least forty other high-impact tax strategies I use and recommend. A qualified professional who knows these rules can reduce your tax burden substantially.

Real Life Stories

Craig Golightly receives income from a job, a small business, and a rental. He self-prepared his taxes for years. He was always super conservative with his returns because he worried about getting audited. As a result, he was always overpaying on his taxes. After hiring a CPA, he began saving thousands of dollars a year in taxes.

One year he received a notification from the IRS that there were discrepancies in his return. As a result, the IRS was asking for an additional $2,750 in taxes. Craig said, "A few years ago I would have panicked and just paid the first notice. Now I called my accountant, and we reviewed my business records for that year and found quite a few items I had self-filed incorrectly. I was not afraid to have my tax advisor review and amend my return. No more self-preparation for me."

After his CPA amended his returns, the IRS sent him another letter saying that, instead of him owing additional taxes, he now had a refund of $2,702 coming back to him. In addition to the refund, they also paid him $117.59 in interest. Craig said, "Having a qualified adviser who knows the tax law helped legally put cash back into my pockets."

Jim Hori is a dentist who was looking for ways to free up cash. He started by working with an expert CPA to see if he could save money on taxes. His CPA discovered that Jim had suffered an investment loss from a bad investment. The man who had promoted the investment had gone to jail. Jim's previous CPA had told him that he could only deduct $3,000 a year on that loss. But his new CPA explained to him that, because the man he invested with went to jail, the law allowed him to deduct the whole loss of $200,000. This one thing saved Jim $100,000 in taxes. It pays to have a competent professional in your corner!

Analyze Investments for Hidden Fees

There are tons of hidden fees in conventional investments such as 401(k)s and IRAs, which most people aren't even aware of. Even a 1 percent fee can end up being hundreds of thousands of dollars over thirty years.

Fees on investments can consist of the following (usually, not all of these would apply in one case, and this is not an all-inclusive list):

- **Management Fee for a Money Manager:** Typically in the 1 to 1.5 percent range.
- **Expense Ratios:** For mutual funds or exchange-traded funds, 1 to 2 percent depending on the fund.
- **Administrative Fees:** In the case of a 401(k), 403(b), or other similar plans, there are typically fees for the plan itself. Most of these fees should be covered by the plan sponsor

(the business), but some can also be passed on to the participants in the plan.

- **Loads:** Mutual funds, especially A, B, and C shares, have sales loads up front, on the back end when you sell, or both. These can be as high as 5 percent or more. This is in addition to the expense ratio on the funds and is typically a commission paid to the broker who sold the shares of the funds to you.

- **Miscellaneous Fees:** There are other fees, like 12b-1 fees (mutual fund marketing fees that you pay for), which may seem nominal but especially have an impact when added on to the above fees.

Another consideration here is that, if you have loans and investments, you might be earning less on your interest with your investments than you're paying on the loans. By paying off the loan, the loan interest is a guaranteed cost that you could free up and save versus taking risks to try to earn it with your investments.

Become a Money Master

After showing some ways to boost your cash flow without reducing your spending, I want to stress that it's still important that you learn to be financially disciplined. Building your 5 Day Weekend will require concerted effort.

Money should be your obedient, diligent servant, not your master. Money must work for you, rather than you working for money. What you need to do is to change how you relate to money.

To accomplish this, here are three vital financial disciplines you must master:

1. Pay Yourself First

By utilizing this principle, you can become the master of money. There are many methods to develop this fiscal discipline. One method I used when I was starting out was mailing an invoice to myself every week. It was a constant reminder to pay myself first.

By paying yourself first, you build a liquid "war chest" that can be accessed to take advantage of opportunities. Paying yourself first promotes healthy financial habits and becomes a powerful motivator.

2. Master the 5-Second Rule

The 5-Second Rule is the accountability discipline of eliminating impulse buys. Before making any purchase, pause and ask yourself if you really need this item now? Can you wait six months or a year? Do you really need to spend the money? Is this purchase logical? Will the value of the item outweigh the cost? Most people spend indiscriminately and never ponder the consequences.

3. Leave Your Credit Card at Home

This approach ensures that you spend only what you have in your debit account. It encourages wise money management practices. When you spend with your debit card, you feel it more. When you have eliminated the majority of bad debt and fully grasped the 5-Second Rule, you can upgrade your card selection to include credit cards.

By freeing up cash that is being lost in taxes, interest, insurance costs, investment fees, and undisciplined habits, you have more to work with to build your 5 Day Weekend.

> "Watch the costs and the profits will take care of themselves."
> — ANDREW CARNEGIE

CHAPTER 8

CAPTURE WEALTH

O nce you've plugged the leaks in your financial bucket, you're prepared to start building a foundation of wealth.

The key to capturing and creating wealth is to make it automatic. Ideally, you should set up automatic transfers to sweep a percentage of your income into a savings account before you get a chance to spend it. This way you'll grow wealthier, even if you drain your spending account to the bottom every month. (We recommend depositing savings in two accounts.)

Saving automatically is even more important when times are tight, because it forces you to be resourceful and your wealth still continues to grow. Also, by automatically transferring a percentage of your income, rather than a set amount, the amount that goes into your accounts grows with your income. You grow wealth faster and faster as time goes on.

Eliminating high-interest debt should be your first priority. Once that has been taken care of, set up the following accounts with automatic transfers.

Capture Wealth Accounts

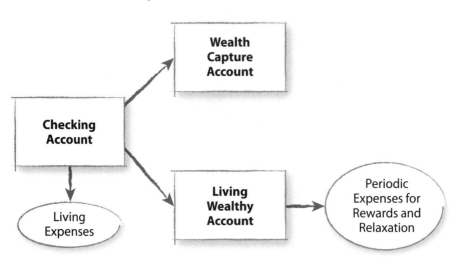

Account #1: Wealth Capture Account

A Wealth Capture Account is a way to automatically grow wealthier every month. It works like this: Create a sweep account with your main checking account—wherever your income is deposited each month. A sweep account allows you to automatically transfer a percentage of your checking account into a savings account or other account. Set up an automatic transfer to sweep a percentage of your income, on the day it is deposited, into a savings account. This is your Wealth Capture Account.

Ideally, we recommend that you save 15 percent of your net income (after all deductions and taxes) into your Wealth Capture Account. If that sounds like a lot, don't worry. You can start smaller and work your way up to 15 percent. The important thing is that you're growing wealthier every month.

For example, if you know $3,000 will be deposited on the 1st and 15th of every month, you can set up an automatic 15 percent ($450) transfer into your Wealth Capture Account on the 2nd and 16th of each month. With this example, you'll have $900 transferred into your Wealth Capture Account after the first month, $2,700 after the third month, and $10,800 after one year — all automatically.

Your Wealth Capture Account serves as your emergency fund, peace of mind fund, and opportunity fund for accumulating capital with which to invest.

Why Save 15 Percent?

Fifteen percent isn't an arbitrary number. It's a percentage based on several factors that must be taken into consideration to build sustainable wealth. Specifically:

- **3 Percent for Taxes:** Have you ever been surprised by a tax bill that you couldn't cover? Your Wealth Capture Account takes care of that.
- **3 Percent for Inflation:** Inflation, which erodes the value of your money, generally averages about 3 percent (conservatively).
- **3 Percent for Technological Change:** As technology improves, the costs generally fall, but we tend to buy it more frequently.
- **3 Percent for Propensity to Consume:** What starts off as a luxury quickly becomes a necessity. For example, it wasn't that long ago that no one had a cell phone. Now everyone does — even homeless people. Once people get used to a certain lifestyle, they rarely are willing to give it up.
- **3 Percent for Planned Obsolescence:** Household goods and appliances break down and need to be replaced.

By planning and saving for these predictable and unavoidable things, we're able to build wealth even in spite of them.

Account #2: Living Wealthy Account

The purpose of this account is to save money for guilt-free spending on eating out, shopping, vacations, courtside tickets, or whatever luxury brings you value, helps you relax, or restores your energy. We recommend that you save 3 percent of your income in your Living Wealthy Account.

Don't underestimate the value of this account. The point of it is to allow you to splurge a little even while building wealth. If you budget too tightly and never allow yourself enjoyment, it's not sustainable. It gets old quickly. This account helps you maintain a healthy, productive, relaxed mindset while you're working toward your 5 Day Weekend.

When you combine these two accounts, ideally you should be saving 18 percent of your income. So what do you do with the money you're accumulating?

A Big Step

When you set these accounts up, you've made a significant move toward your 5 Day Weekend. Now you're ready to build on your accounts to maximize your investments. In the next chapter, we will show you a way to use the cash you build in your Wealth Capture Account.

> **"A goal without a plan is just a wish."**
> — LARRY ELDER

CHAPTER 9

I recommend the Rockefeller Formula to maximize your Wealth Capture Account. It was created by Garrett and his team to build wealth consistently and automatically. It provides a safe, secure, and liquid way to save your money for your business or investments.

The Rockefeller Formula allows you to live comfortably now without any fear of running out of money. You create a perpetual family bank as a way to keep the money together and growing.

The Rockefeller family used a similar system to grow and protect generational wealth. Many other wealthy people and families use the same principles and tools.

The best vehicle for this account is a properly structured and overfunded whole life insurance contract, a plan Garrett calls Cash Flow Insurance. You funnel money into this insurance contract from your Wealth Capture Account.

Rockefeller Formula

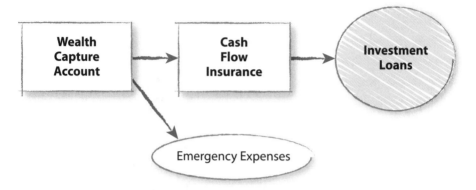

Big Picture Overview

- You set up a whole life insurance policy with the ability to add cash above the minimum required premium.
- Then, using money from your Wealth Capture Account, you overfund it by paying much more than the minimum payments. This builds your cash value quickly and enables you to take advantage of the living benefits of permanent life insurance.
- Once your policy has built enough cash value—usually after one or two years—you can take out a loan against your policy at any time and for any amount up to 90-plus percent of the cash value. Notice that we said "against," not "from." Your loan isn't taken out of your cash value. Rather, your cash value is used as collateral. Therefore, your policy continues to grow as if you hadn't taken out a loan at all, because you are not actually taking any money out of the cash value of the policy.

Benefits You Gain

You can use policy loans to access cash for any purpose (while your balance continues to grow). You can also use them to pay for your kids' education, finance your own home, buy cash flow investments, or even pay off loans. These loans from your "bank" are private, do not have a specific payback period, and do not require a credit check (or even a good credit score for that matter).

You can use your policy loans to purchase investments. We recommend that you pay back the loans as quickly as possible. But you don't just pay back the principal of the loan—you pay it back with interest. The interest you pay should be at a rate that you would have been charged by a bank using a traditional loan, not the rate you were actually charged from your policy loan. This grows the money inside your policy even more quickly, because you're paying yourself interest instead of paying interest to a bank.

You never have to rush to pay back the loan. In fact, most insurance companies don't care if you miss a payment, or several payments, or even if you pay them back at all—because if you don't pay them back, the balance is simply deducted when your death benefit is paid out. With that said, we recommend that you pay back the loan quickly so you can use the money for future loans on investments.

Also, borrowing from your Cash Flow Insurance policy will never affect your credit, since there are no such things as late payments. Additionally, if the loan is for your business, in most cases the interest you pay on it is tax deductible.

Source of Investment Cash

Cash Flow Insurance is the perfect wealth creation tool for entrepreneurs and investors. Your money isn't locked up in the stock market until you're age 59½—like it is with 401(k)s and IRAs. Instead it's always available to borrow from, in order to accelerate your business growth or to purchase investments.

For example, suppose you find a great real estate deal that can make you a lot of money in a short period but requires $20,000 down. If you don't have that in cash, you can borrow it from your Cash Flow Insurance policy with no credit check, extremely low interest rates, and no timetable for repayment. Then, you can use the cash flow from rent to pay back the loan.[4]

Deposits you make into your personal Cash Flow Insurance policy never lose value, providing you with capital preservation without risking principal. Your cash value is not affected by market volatility if the economy "crashes" again. It protects you against litigation, so you never have to worry about losing your money due to a lawsuit or bankruptcy (protection varies by state). Your account is a contract, so you know exactly what your guaranteed returns are. And since this is a private contract, it is not regulated like government-sponsored retirement plans.

Your wealth grows automatically as your account enjoys tax-favored growth and takes full advantage of compounding interest. The steady, guaranteed return historically averages about 4 percent, while non-guaranteed dividends can add an additional boost to your cash value by 1 percent or more.

As a business owner, Garrett is constantly looking at opportunities, and using his Cash Flow Insurance policy allows him to take advantage of those opportunities. Garrett has used his Cash Flow Insurance policy many times since 1998. He's used it to buy into businesses, to pay off real estate and credit cards, and to invest in a video recording studio for his business. By using his policy to invest, the money he has earned from investments has paid for the insurance costs of the policy.

Real Life Stories

Troy Remelski is a business owner who set up a Cash Flow Insurance policy to capture and create wealth. He found a house that would require a six-figure remodel but could make him a lot of money. He said, "Before using Cash Flow Insurance, I would've been left with a difficult decision about the best way to pay for the remodel. I'd have to choose between putting money away for retirement and delaying the remodel, or not fully funding my retirement to make sure I could cover the remodeling costs. By using life insurance, it was a no-brainer: Put the money into insurance and take a loan out for anything I couldn't pay immediately from cash flow. Now, my money is working for me in both the policy and the equity appreciation we will gain from the home's newly remodeled value. And, my stress level was much lower because I knew I could always loan myself more money if we hit any unexpected costs along the way."

THE ROCKEFELLER FORMULA **81**

Jeff Chamberlain is a chiropractor who was struggling with just over $86,000 in business debt from a business line of credit, an X-ray machine, and a credit card, which were costing him about $3,000 a month in payments. He said, "I hate being in debt. I hate feeling like someone else or something has more control than I do. It felt like a large weight on my shoulders that was always in the back of my mind."

He purchased and overfunded a Cash Flow Insurance policy. Then, he took $86,000 out of his IRA, which had no guarantee of stable returns, and used it to pay off all his business debt as a personal loan from him to the business. Next, his business started paying him back the $3,000 a month he had been paying to his creditors. But now, the payments went into his Cash Flow Insurance account. Jeff said, "My Cash Flow Insurance account not only earns a minimum of 4 percent guaranteed, but also creates a cash flow source. I can now be my own bank whenever I choose, under my own terms."

Important Considerations

It is important that you properly fund and commit to your Cash Flow Insurance policy. If you were to abandon this early on, you could lose money due to the up-front costs of the life insurance policy. Or, if it is designed improperly, the insurance costs could be too high, and it could take too long before you have access to your money. When you set up your policy it's important that you review it carefully and ask questions to make sure it includes all the benefits we have outlined.

Other Cash Resources

Whole life insurance is not the only vehicle you can use to save money and borrow from using your cash as collateral, but no savings vehicle has the same benefits as Cash Flow Insurance. Retirement plans could work, because you can borrow from them—but there is no guarantee of principal without moving to a money market at a very low interest rate. There's also no death benefit. There are strict limits on how much you borrow and on the schedule for paying the loan back, plus there's no option to pay back more than the loan amount and thereby capture interest.

Savings accounts at a bank could work, but they are currently paying less than 1 percent interest. Certificates of Deposit and certain types of bonds offer better returns than savings accounts and are fairly well guaranteed, but there would be penalties if you were to liquidate. In some cases you can get a line of credit or loan against a CD, but this still lacks key advantages since it will have a lower interest rate.

We also don't like leaving money in a CD or a money market because it's subject to taxes, to creditors, and to low interest rates. Cash Flow Insurance offers a consistent, guaranteed return, along with powerful tax advantages and significant liquidity. With Cash Flow Insurance, it doesn't matter if interest rates go up or down, because when you have your cash value and your dividends have been paid, you are guaranteed a minimum interest rate. That means you won't have capital depreciation (you won't lose principal). You'll have stability and predictability.

Moreover, if an insurance company goes out of business, your money is much more likely to be secure compared with accounts in other institutions. When Executive Life went out of business in the 1980s, no policyholder lost money. Another insurance company acquired all the accounts. Even if an insurance company goes out of business and another company doesn't buy it out, every state has guarantees on death benefits and the cash value in policies. Mutual life insurance companies with A-type ratings are much more stable and predictable than any other financial institution.

Getting Started

A Cash Flow Insurance contract should be established once you have at least three months of expenses set aside in your Wealth Capture Account. At that point, you would funnel money from your Wealth Capture Account into your Cash Flow Insurance policy, which is set up carefully and strategically to maximize the benefits.

Meanwhile, you keep a portion of your Wealth Capture Account in savings, separate from your life insurance policy, as your peace of mind fund. You want this account to hold at least six months of salary. That way, if you lose your job, you can cover debt obligations and living expenses.

For more information on the Rockefeller Formula, visit 5DayWeekend.com.
Code: P3

Think Wealthy

If you want to become wealthy, you must learn to think wealthy. Some of the most powerful and wealthy people of the past century have relied on the power of the Rockefeller Formula using Cash Flow Insurance. Along with the Rockefeller family, that elite list includes people and groups such as Walt Disney, J.C. Penney, Ray Kroc, the Rothschild family, John F. Kennedy, and Franklin D. Roosevelt. Senator John McCain secured initial campaign financing for his 2008 presidential campaign by using his life insurance policy as collateral.[5]

The rich play by a different set of rules. The solution is simple: If you want to become rich, you must invest like the rich and start your own family bank.

> **"Money is plentiful for those who understand the simple laws which govern its acquisition."**
> —GEORGE S. CLASON

CHAPTER 10

ROCK-SOLID
FINANCIAL
BASELINE

The purpose of this first step of the 5 Day Weekend plan is to get your financial house in order—to establish a solid foundation from which you can safely create more income and invest.

Below are the milestones Garrett and I recommend you achieve before moving on to the next steps. Achieving these milestones will give you a healthy financial baseline and provide you with much greater safety and security.

1. Get Properly Protected

Auto Insurance

Suppose you were to cause an accident. The other driver is disabled and can't work for six months. Would your current coverage cover this situation? Do you understand the different components of your policy enough to know?

Few people understand the liability limits on their auto insurance, which covers bodily injury, as well as compensates for uninsured and underinsured claims. Suppose someone else hits you and you're disabled for six months or longer. He only has $25,000 of coverage, but you make $150,000 a year. Assuming your limits are high enough, your underinsured coverage would make up the difference.

It's important to understand the difference between property value (cars, computers, etc.) and human life value (meaning your potential to produce). Strangely, most people insure their property value but are woefully underinsured when it comes to their human life value. What's more important: Replacing your income if you are disabled, or replacing your car if it gets damaged?

Homeowner's Insurance

If you were to have a liability claim on your homeowner's insurance, have you fully transferred your risk and protected your assets?

Is your liability limit the same as your car insurance? Do you have the proper amount of property coverage, including full replacement (as opposed to actual) value? Do you have a video inventory of your belongings offsite? Is your deductible set at the right amount? Have you maximized your multi-policy discount in coordination with your auto insurance?

Excess Liability/Umbrella Coverage

An umbrella policy is absolutely essential for proper protection. Umbrella insurance is extra liability insurance designed to protect you from major claims and lawsuits. It can also reduce your premium on your car and homeowner's coverage, if coordinated properly. For example, you can lower your liability coverage on your auto and homeowner policies to the minimum requirements, and then use the umbrella policy to cover catastrophic losses.

Disability Insurance

If you become disabled, it may only be temporary. But even temporary disability can have a devastating impact on your family. Could you handle having no income for three months or longer? How much sense does it make to protect your car and not protect yourself and your income?

Medical Insurance

Do you have the right type of medical insurance for your situation? Do you have the proper deductibles to minimize premiums and yet keep adequate peace of mind that your benefits are not out of reach compared to your liquidity and frequency of use with the policy?

Life Insurance

If you were to die today, would your life insurance replace your economic value and ensure the same lifestyle your family currently enjoys?

Don't consider life insurance as a big lump sum that is paid when you die. Rather, consider how much income that lump sum can produce over your family's life. You'll never find a widower or widow who felt like he or she had too much coverage.

Do you understand the different types of insurance and is your policy right for you? Do you have the proper beneficiary assignment with your policy?

Estate Planning

Estate planning determines what happens to your assets when you pass away. But equally important is the perpetuation of your values, philosophy, vision, and contribution. A proper estate plan maximizes your legacy—both financial and personal.

Do you have a properly documented will? Do you have a properly executed trust? Do you have a Power of Attorney set up in case you are incapacitated and cannot make decisions? Does your plan account for transferring human life value assets (values, philosophy, and contribution)?

Liquidity: Checking and Savings

Are you confident in the solvency and quality of your bank? Do you have six months' worth of expenses in a liquid account that is totally safe? Do you have at least one month of expenses in cash on hand and another month in precious metals?

2. Maximize Your Financial Efficiency

Debt

Have you applied the Cash Flow Index to all your loans? Do you have a clear plan for eliminating all of your inefficient loans as quickly and efficiently as possible?

Loans

Have you negotiated the best interest rate on your loans? Have you maximized tax advantages and savings by keeping your loan interest tax deductible? Do you have a detailed and coordinated plan to pay off loans you'd like to eliminate?

Accounting and Taxes

Do you have adequate and effective tracking and bookkeeping systems to measure your production?

Are you proactively strategizing throughout the year to save on taxes? Have you reviewed previous tax returns with someone other than your current accountant to see if you can amend returns to recapture overpayment of taxes? Is your business set up optimally from a tax and legal perspective? Do you have an exit strategy for your retirement plans, stocks, real estate, or other investments to minimize the tax consequences?

3. Maximize Your Production

Your balance sheet shows your assets versus liabilities to determine whether you have equity (net worth) or debt (more liabilities than assets). The key is to produce more than you consume so that you are creating a positive balance on your personal balance sheet.

Are you creating more value in the world than you take? Are you clear on your passion, purpose, and values, and does your business/career reflect that clarity? Does your business maximize your talents and knowledge to create value for others?

Rockefeller Formula Cash Flow Insurance

Have you created your own personal banking system to self-finance and capture interest normally paid to banks?

Credit Score

Do you know your credit score? Do you know how to maintain or improve it? A 780-plus credit score can help you lower your interest rates on existing loans or give you greater access to credit, which can be used to increase your production.

> "Everyone has the ability to build a financial ark to survive and flourish in the future."
> —ROBERT KIYOSAKI

Call to Action
Your Debt Free Plan

Your Current Loans

Make a list of all your current loans. For each loan complete its current balance, interest rate, monthly payment, and cash flow index (balance divided by payment).

Organize all your loans (e.g., Visa card, truck loan, mortgage, etc.) in order of lowest to highest Cash Flow Index. This is the order in which you should pay off your loans.

Your Plan to Plug Cash Flow Leaks

What is your current credit score? Your spouse's?
What is your plan for boosting your credit score(s)?
How can you restructure your loans to boost your cash flow?
How can you restructure your insurance to boost your cash flow?
Do you currently have a legal entity (e.g., LLC, S Corp, etc.)? If not, schedule a time to meet with your CPA.

Your Plan to Capture and Create Wealth

To start, what is the amount (% of your income) you commit to saving in a Wealth Capture Account?
Your target date for increasing that to 15 percent?
Your target date to fund your Cash Flow Insurance Policy?

Go to our website to download and print this worksheet at 5DayWeekend.com.
Code: P4

While working on putting your financial house in order, you should also work on increasing your income. The fastest way is with entrepreneurial work. It's time for you to take massive action to build your active income. The purpose of this increased income isn't to upgrade your lifestyle—at least, not just yet. The purpose is to have discretionary funds with which to invest in passive income opportunities.

Entrepreneurialism is the best way to provide you with wealth, cash flow, and tax advantages, and set you up for life. Tax laws also favor the entrepreneur and punish the poor. Regular employee income, savings, and 401(k)s of the middle class and the poor are taxed disproportionately.

CHAPTERS

- **Increase Your Active Income**

- **It Doesn't Take Money**

- **Exploring Entrepreneurial Ideas**

- **Analyze Income Opportunities**

- **Before You Quit Your Job**

- *Call to Action*
  Your Entrepreneurial Income Plan

CHAPTER 11

INCREASE YOUR ACTIVE INCOME

You've been building a solid financial foundation. You're getting out of debt. You're recovering cash you were losing to the IRS, poor investments, poorly structured insurance, and interest. You're able to save more money.

Now, the goal is to increase your active income. This seems counterintuitive, since I've said that the whole goal of the 5 Day Weekend lifestyle is to build passive income. But you're only going to do this initially so you can create discretionary funds with which to invest. It's not true that it takes money to make money, as you'll learn in the next chapter. However, it does take money for most investments. The more you have to invest, the faster you can build your 5 Day Weekend lifestyle.

In this stage, I'm not talking about working longer hours at your job or asking for a raise (although that certainly wouldn't hurt). I'm talking about building entrepreneurial income on the side in ways that give you greater leverage and more opportunity than you can get at your job.

This is a safe approach to entering the waters of entrepreneurship. You're not going to do anything that jeopardizes your finances or family. You're not going to quit your job immediately and hope and pray something works out. You're going to experiment with stuff on the side with minimal investment. You'll learn from what doesn't work and build on what does work.

Start, Experiment, and Learn

If you've never done anything entrepreneurial, understandably you may feel intimidated by the process. You may not know what you're doing. You don't know what will work. You don't know where to start.

The key is to simply start somewhere. Do something. Don't let fear or any lack of knowledge or skill hold you back. Procrastination is a fear fertilizer. Just do something and see what happens.

> "Failure is a bruise, not a tattoo."
>
> —JON SINCLAIR

Some of your experiments will fail. When that happens, since you're experimenting on the side, you don't have to worry that you can't pay your bills. You'll walk away with more knowledge, skill, experience, and wisdom that you can apply to your next venture. And when something does succeed, you'll build on it as long as it makes sense. It may even be profitable enough over time to allow you to quit your job.

Real Life Story

Kyle Moffat was born and raised in Alaska. He's thirty years old and works full time as an oil field production operator at a facility that pumps oil through the Trans-Alaska pipeline. He makes great money and only works five months out of the year, working two weeks on and two weeks off. But no matter how much money he makes at his job and no matter how flexible his schedule, he knows he'll never be truly free working for someone else.

In 2012 he started an online blog called *The Alaska Life*. As an avid outdoorsman and adventurer, he constantly had people asking him what gear to use. So he started the blog as a way to answer people's questions in one place. He had no business plan for it; it was just a hobby. But he was pleasantly surprised when the blog took off and a loyal fan base developed. He started selling branded hats, hoodies, and T-shirts and made $20,000 to $30,000 in gross revenues, just playing around on the side. After a couple of years he had over 250,000 Facebook fans.

> "There are two ways to get to the top of an oak tree. One way is to sit on an acorn and wait; the other way is to climb it."
>
> —KEMMONS WILSON

He started looking for ways to monetize the business even further. After taking online courses on drop shipping, he launched an Amazon drop-shipping business on October 1, 2014, starting with private-labeled GoPro selfie sticks and stainless steel water bottles. He was sweating bullets, wondering if he'd really be able to sell anything, but his first product order was for $6,000. Within eight weeks of launching, he was selling $90,000 per month (sales spiked for the holidays). In 2015, his first full year in business, he made a total of $750,000 in gross revenues. He now routinely makes product orders of $100,000 or more.

Although the business makes between $6,000 and $12,000 per month in profits, Kyle hasn't pocketed any money yet. He's rolling all his profits back into the business to keep the growth going. The business has funded itself. He expects to replace his job income soon.

Kyle told us, "Everyone I work with at my pipeline job makes awesome money for as much time as we work. People here are fat, dumb, and happy. They pour money into their 401(k)s. But there's no real long-term wealth in doing this. I tell people they have to shift their minds. You have to do your own thing because you'll never get ahead if you're just working hourly, even if you're making good money."

Start as Small as Possible

In most cases vision is a good thing. But when you first start something on the side, sometimes vision can actually hold you back. All too often people get scared away from entrepreneurship because they see a vision of how much they have to build, and it feels too overwhelming.

The key is to think in terms of a minimum viable product. Forget about some grandiose scheme that will require a large capital investment, a team, infrastructure, etc. Learn to take things to market with very little if any capital expenditure. Become an expert on a strategy Garrett calls "Win, Then Play." In other words, before you fully commit to a project or opportunity, test its market viability first. Do everything you can to prove market demand before investing a ton of time, money, and energy into it. To use a baseball analogy, you don't have to hit a home run—you just have to make contact with the ball and get on base.

> "Start your first business this way: Begin with the smallest possible project in which someone will pay you money to solve a problem they know they have. Charge less than it's worth and more than it costs you. Repeat. You don't have to wait for perfect or large or revered or amazing. You can start."[6]
>
> —SETH GODIN

Real Life Stories

Stephen Palmer is an author and purpose coach. He wanted to increase his passive income, so he started brainstorming possibilities. Stephen came up with the idea to write and design inspirational "life manifestos" as posters and canvas prints.

He had no idea whether or not he could sell them, however. So instead of investing a bunch of time and money up front, he simply wrote one manifesto, the "Family Manifesto," and paid a graphic designer to design it. He didn't set up a business entity. He didn't have a website. He printed just one copy of his poster so he could take pictures of it framed. He offered it for sale on a daily deals site (similar to Groupon). Based on other products he was seeing on the site, he figured that if he sold at least fifty, the idea would be worth pursuing. Otherwise, he'd drop it and try something else.

He was pleasantly surprised when he sold 392 copies on his first offer. He hurried and printed enough to fulfill those initial orders. Then and only then did he start developing the business. He now has a fully developed e-commerce site offering twelve different manifestos in three different formats, and the business generates thousands of dollars in profits per year with very little time. The only money he invested up front out of his own pocket was to pay a graphic designer for his first poster. Since his first offer, the business has paid for itself. Any other investment he's had to make has come from poster sales, not out of his own pocket.

In 2002 Dan McCoy was working full time as an electrical engineer for a large aerospace corporation. He knew how to build computers and was frustrated with all the "crapware," as he put it, that popular computer companies like Dell were putting onto their computers. He saw a niche where he could be of value. He started building personal computers that were more streamlined, higher quality, and faster than what most people were getting in the marketplace and selling them on the side. He also focused on providing great service to his customers.

It started out just as a hobby for him, but the business grew. Over time he began expanding his services. By 2009 his side business had advanced to providing consulting and managed IT services for small businesses (although he was still working full time). He noticed that there was something wrong with the standard model of the industry. Companies only paid him and other service providers like him when their computers went down. So what incentive did they have to keep the computers up and running? He saw an opportunity to fix this model.

Instead of just charging an hourly rate for fixing things when they crashed, he switched to a recurring revenue model. Companies would pay him a flat fee to do proactive monitoring and keep their computers and their networks functional. It was a great value proposition for his clients and a better fit for his business. Over time, he completely shifted his model. Within one year he had over $80,000 per year in recurring revenues coming in.

In September of 2010, his company censured him for having his side business and checking emails on company computers—even though he had never cheated the time clock. They gave him three days without pay. His daughter was a year old and his son was nine years old. He spent those three days at home playing with his daughter. It made him realize how much of his children's lives he had missed, and he vowed he wasn't going to miss any more. He knew it was time to make a change.

When he returned to work, his decision was even more solidified because the company put stringent requirements on him. He said, "They had me locked down to specific hours on the time clock. They tied me to time instead of value and took my freedom to create value away. They were trying to control me, and I hated it."

Dan followed Garrett's steps for freeing up cash flow that I've outlined. He freed up enough cash to make it possible for him to quit his job, take a 60 percent pay cut, and still take care of his family. He also worked hard when he was off the clock to build his business and expand his customer base. His last day of working for someone else was January 14, 2011.

Within one year of quitting his job, he had more than doubled his company's revenues. Since then, his revenues have increased by more than four times and his profits have tripled. Eighty-five percent of his business is recurring revenue, and his gross profits are between 50 and 60 percent. He has two full-time employees and a team of more than sixty other people to whom he outsources work. He now has the freedom to do what he wants, when he wants. And it all started as a hobby on the side.

We asked Dan what advice he would give to someone who wants to transition from a job to a business. He answered, "First of all, do what brings you joy. There's nothing worse than starting a business and hating it. It has to be fun for you. Do something you're passionate about and where you can make a difference for other people. Without passion you are grazing through life as if nothing really matters. Also, be clear about your endgame. Know where you want to be in five to ten years."

Continuous Improvement

You can start small and experiment without taking on too much risk. But by no means should this be interpreted as acting timidly. Building your 5 Day Weekend requires boldness and action.

It's about commitment. It's about steady and sustained improvement, versus sporadic effort that fizzles out. The term I like for it is "kaizen," which is a Japanese word referring to the process of continuous improvement. The idea of kaizen is that big results come from many small changes accumulated over time.

> "Spend each day trying to be a little wiser than you were when you woke up. Step by step you get ahead. You build discipline by preparing for fast spurts."
> —CHARLIE MUNGER

My challenge to you is to increase your income by 3 percent each month, at least for the first couple of years of your 5 Day Weekend journey. This becomes a 38.4 percent increase in income at the end of your first year. By year two, you will have achieved a 97.4 percent increase, almost doubling your income. For example, suppose you're currently earning $3,000 per month. Watch how this can work:

Year 1

- Month 1: $3,000 × 3% = $90
- Month 2: $3,090 × 3% = $92.70
- Month 3: $3,182.70 × 3% = $95.48
- Month 4: $3,278.18 × 3% = $98.35
- Month 5: $3,376.53 × 3% = $101.30
- Month 6: $3,477.83 × 3% = $104.33
- At six months: $3,477.83 (16% increase)
- At twelve months: $4,152.70 (38.4% increase)
- At twenty-four months: $5,920.77 (97.4% increase)

This approach essentially "gamifies" your experience and gives you an incentive to keep improving over time. Each month's returns compete with the previous month's, thus perpetuating the gamification process. Feel free to experiment and increase by more than 3 percent per month, but do everything you can to hit that minimum. At the very least, set a specific goal for how much you want to increase your income each month. Have a specified target to shoot for versus just hoping you'll improve.

Maintaining this increase is easier in the beginning years, when you're not making as much money. Over time it can become harder, but the principle still applies: Never stop improving, never stop striving to increase your income month over month.

> "The smallest of actions is always better than the noblest of intentions."
> —ROBIN SHARMA

CHAPTER 12

IT DOESN'T TAKE MONEY

After getting divorced, Monica moved from New York to Utah with her three children. She arrived in Utah with literally no money, and nothing but her children and the contents of two suitcases to her name. She found a job working for a gift shop in the mall and was able to provide for the basics.

But Monica knew she was capable of more. She was an amazing cook and loved everything to do with food and nutrition. She'd always had a dream: to "love people through food," as she puts it. She wanted to help people eat healthier, better-tasting food, yet she thought being self-employed or starting a business was risky. Everyone around her gave the standard advice to get a good job with good benefits.

Fortunately, Monica didn't give up. She saw others successfully doing what she wanted to do, so she knew it was possible.

She started by providing meals for individual clients (Garrett was one of her first). Because she did such an incredible job, word quickly spread, and she created enough relationships and gained enough clients to quit her other job and focus on her dream full time. One year after she quit her job, she was earning her previous annual salary in eight days.

Monica and many others like her are living proof that it doesn't take money to make money. What it does take is initiative, determination, and value creation. Money is nothing but evidence of value creation. It has no intrinsic value. It's a representation of value exchange between people. It's the product of solving problems, alleviating pain, and creating joy for people.

> "I've never been poor, only broke. Being poor is a frame of mind. Being broke is only a temporary situation."
>
> —MIKE TODD

Never let the lack of money stop you from putting yourself out there and creating value. Everything you need to make more money is between your ears. You don't get paid by the hour. You get paid based on the value you bring to the hour. Learn to develop more value to your hours.

Three Types of Capital: Garrett's Value Equation

Most people think they need financial capital to start a business. The reality is that there are three types of capital, and financial capital is the least important.

Mental Capital

Mental capital allows you to create value for others and can simply be defined as what you know. This could include your skill sets, education, experiences, insights, or any other type of knowledge. And it almost always involves specialization. No one can be an expert on every topic, but you can be a top expert on one topic. We strongly recommend that you add to your mental capital every day by spending time learning about your area of expertise.

> **"If you think education is expensive, try ignorance."**
> —HARVEY MACKAY

Relationship Capital

Relationship capital refers to the people you have a connection with, create value for, or who know and trust you. Helping people solve problems or being of service builds relationship equity, or goodwill. High-performing people are protective of their relationships, and they typically don't hang around people who don't add value. Important relationships should include mentors, teachers, and others who are contributing to increasing your mental capital.

You've heard of OPM—other people's money—and this is certainly part of relationship capital. But it also includes OPN (other people's networks), OPT (other people's time), and more. You don't have to rely on your own money, connections, time, or energy. You can build relationships with people who personally own or have access to the resources you need.

Financial Capital

Financial capital is just what it seems—money you have access to. Financial capital expands when you create more value than you consume. It's a by-product of how effectively you utilize your mental capital to create value for people.

> **"You are only one relationship or one idea away from your next level of prosperity."**
> —GARRETT GUNDERSON

And remember, financial capital doesn't have to be money you personally own. It can be owned by others with whom you have relationship capital.

As you're able to increase your three forms of capital simultaneously, they will have an exponential effect on one another. This will enable your capacity to create value and therefore bolster your reserves and capabilities even further. Simply put, the more you have to offer, the more you are able to receive in return.

If you're struggling with money, it's not a money problem. Instead, you don't have enough of the right mental or relationship capital. In short, your Value Equation is broken. The Value Equation looks like this:

Mental Capital × Relationship Capital = Financial Capital

If you want more money (i.e., financial capital), you have to increase your mental capital, your relationship capital, or both. You're always just an idea or relationship away from a major breakthrough.

Leverage and Maximize Your Current Assets

Everywhere you turn, you find people waiting. Waiting for a better job opportunity. Waiting for more money. Waiting for the stars to align. Wishing for more time, more resources.

But waiting can simply be an excuse to let fear rule your life. You're not lacking anything—in fact, if you have eyes that see, you have way more resources available to you than you may think. What do you have right now in this moment that can be used and leveraged to create value for others? What are you waiting for?

> "Start where you are. Use what you have. Do what you can."
>
> —ARTHUR ASHE

Garrett and I both started with no money. Neither of us was born with silver spoons in our mouths. We've had to learn how to take initiative and be innovative and resourceful. We've both learned from personal experience that it doesn't take money to make money—it just takes a willingness to hustle and to learn from your mistakes.

My Story

One rainy afternoon, when I was ten years old, my brother Jim and I were watching a television documentary about Jimi Hendrix. I thought Hendrix was really cool. He was incredibly innovative and unlike any other guitarist the world had heard. A spark began to flicker, which would soon burst into a passionate inner fire.

I had started taking guitar lessons at age ten and rapidly progressed. By the age of twelve, I had surpassed the talents of my first guitar tutor. By thirteen, I was practicing guitar for three hours every day after school. I dedicated my life to music.

I started teaching guitar lessons. I advertised on the notice boards of music shops. Potential students would come to our house and ask about guitar lessons. They would ask, "Is Nik Halik here?" When I said I was Nik, they'd laugh; I was half their age and size. If they needed convincing, I'd challenge them to give me a chance and jam a few guitar riffs to show them what I was capable of.

Soon I knew more about playing guitar than my second tutor. My development as a guitarist was relentless. I had progressed through several tutors by the age of fifteen and eventually ran out of tutors in my hometown of Melbourne, Australia.

Now I had more than fifty students, some of whom were performing as professional musicians. I was charging up to $25 an hour, a tidy sum of money for a teenage boy, and that was giving me the capital to upgrade my ownership of more expensive guitars and amplification equipment. I also hired five other instructors and paid them $10 an hour, while I pocketed $15 from each hour-long lesson. That was my first experience with leverage.

> "The brave do not live forever, but the cautious do not live at all."
>
> —MEG CABOT

By the age of seventeen, I had saved $30,000. I used this money to fund my first big move. I started making plans to relocate to Los Angeles in the U.S. to study guitar and music composition with the world's most talented musicians. My dream was to become a great guitarist and performing musician.

I earned a scholarship to the famous Guitar Institute of Technology (GIT), the world's most innovative school of contemporary music and part of the Musicians Institute in Hollywood, California. It offered a comprehensive, hands-on education in contemporary music performance. GIT (now Musicians Institute) is the equivalent to studying law at Harvard University or studying science and technology at MIT.

I moved to Hollywood, California, in my late teens, to study at GIT. It was an awe-inspiring gathering of the world's greatest musicians. The institute was open 24/7 with more than 300 of the world's upcoming musical students in attendance.

My decision to leave Australia was all about being inspired, to feel more alive and to fuel unbridled energy into my life. My dream of being mentored by the world's elite musicians provided the creative spark I needed. Not long after arriving in LA, I formed my first rock band. We spent over a decade touring with some of the biggest rock bands at the time, and I had a blast living the rock guitarist lifestyle.

The whole experience provided a foundation of knowledge and understanding that would lead to much bigger and better things. I learned that I could create value with what I had. There was nothing stopping me from earning a living on my own terms. I didn't need money to start — I just needed a dream and a place to start. We either live to accomplish our own dreams or to be used as a resource to accomplish someone else's.

Garrett's Story

When I was fifteen years old my parents told me that if I got good grades, they'd give me my dad's '75 Chevy pickup. Looking forward to that, I spent hours detailing the truck. My dad was impressed with my work. He worked at a coal mine, and when one of the bosses came into town, he had me detail one of the company vehicles.

This gave me the idea to start my first business detailing cars. I leveraged my relationship capital with my dad to talk to his boss and get a contract to detail all the surface vehicles at the coal mine. At that time I had almost no financial capital. With what little I had — money I had earned by mowing lawns and babysitting — I bought an electric buffer and a few other supplies.

After getting the contract with the coal mine, I went to the local credit union (where my mom worked). The credit union needed detailing for cars it repossessed. I spoke with the president directly and got a contract with him. I also spread the word to everyone I knew, and I got really good at getting referrals. I reinvested my profits to print my logo on air fresheners and little garbage bags that I would leave in the vehicles after I cleaned them.

As a teenager I honestly didn't know how to price my services. All I knew was what the local car dealership was charging, and it seemed like a ton of money to me. So I started undercutting their prices and charging $30 per vehicle. Over time I raised my prices to between $50 and $75, depending on the vehicle. But I was still cheaper than anyone else, and I was happy because at that time it felt like a lot of money.

I hired several employees and paid them $10 an hour. One of them was the son of a well-connected dentist in town. He brought me tons of new clients, and I gave him a commission for anyone he brought. I was easily making about $20 an hour, back when the minimum wage was about $5. Plus, I was earning income from the work my employees were doing, and I could set my own hours. Not a bad gig for a teenager.

I asked teachers and others to teach me how to run financials. Because of their mentoring, I learned how to do basic income and balance sheets. There's a lesson here: Most people don't reach out and ask for help out of embarrassment, or because they think people won't help. But people really are willing to help—especially if you learn to create value for them.

> "Be strong enough to stand alone, smart enough to know when you need help, and brave enough to ask for it."
>
> —MARK AMEND

I ran the business until I went to college. Shortly before going to college, I won the SBA (Small Business Administration) Young Entrepreneur of the Year and Governor's Entrepreneur awards from my state, which came with a $5,000 prize. I used that money to pay for financial licensing and software—the start of my career in financial services.

In short, I started where I was with what I had. I built from one level to the next. At each level I made more money, and I was able to use that as seed capital for my next venture.

Be Resourceful

If you believe the problem that's holding you back is a lack of resources, you haven't accurately defined the problem.

Your entrepreneurial success won't be determined by the amount of resources you can accumulate. Rather, it will be determined by your resourcefulness. The dictionary defines resourcefulness as "having the ability to find quick and clever ways to overcome difficulties." Resourcefulness includes your imagination and creativity, your curiosity and passion, your resolve and determination. It encompasses the utterly unique way that you view and interact with the world—the problems only you see and the solutions only you can create.

There is no such thing as un-resourceful people, only un-resourceful mindsets. You're not lacking anything you need to succeed. Everything you need is already inside you, just awaiting activation by your unwavering commitment to a goal. Every resource you ever need will come to you as you commit wholeheartedly, work diligently, think creatively, and initiate boldly.

> "Doing what you love is the cornerstone of having abundance in your life."
> —WAYNE DYER

CHAPTER 13

EXPLORING ENTREPRENEURIAL IDEAS

The world has changed drastically and fundamentally. In the Information Age, technology, communication, and a global economy have democratized opportunity like never before. I call myself a "cyber gypsy" because the investments I teach can be made from anywhere on the planet on a smartphone. The days of having to work in a cubicle are over. It's no longer necessary. Even if you're working in an office job, telecommuting opportunities are expanding.

You've never had a greater opportunity to start a business with very little or even no up-front cash. There are literally limitless ways you can leverage new technological tools to start something with nothing but a little time and effort.

Here are just a few ideas for you to explore:

Personal Services

As with a job, with personal services you're trading your time for money. This is not where you want to be long-term, but it's a great place to start, for a few reasons. First, the idea is to do something on the side to supplement your income and build discretionary investment income. Second, there's a possibility that what you do here could make you more money than you're making in your regular job. In this case, you could quit your job and be in a better place financially. Third, there's a possibility that whatever you build could be expanded and leveraged. You may want to hire employees to replace your role and expand what you started into a full-fledged business. Regardless, the process can give you vital experience and valuable lessons.

Here are a few possibilities:

Freelancing

The freelance industry is booming like never before, causing massive cultural and economic shifts. There are currently an estimated 53 million Americans doing freelance work. This represents around 34 percent of the U.S. workforce. Forbes estimates that this percentage will increase to over 50 percent by 2020. Freelance opportunities are available for everything from graphic design to writing, marketing to web development, and project management to accounting.

As with any entrepreneurial venture, to succeed as a freelancer you'll need to learn how to market effectively. Marketing and selling yourself are among the most important skills you need to learn to develop a 5 Day Weekend lifestyle anyway, so it's perfect.

Fiverr and Upwork

One way to market freelance services is to offer them on online marketplaces, such as Fiverr.com and Upwork.com. You offer your services, and people who need them can find you from all across the world. At the time of this writing, Fiverr lists more than three million services on its site, with costs ranging from $5 to $500.[7]

Service Businesses

This could be anything you can do right now with very little up-front investment, such as window cleaning, lawn care, cutting hair, painting, or pet care.

The caveat here is that you don't want to get trapped in a self-employed situation with no or little possibility for eventual leverage, such that you're not making enough money to get ahead.

Building Mobile Apps

One of the most cutting-edge frontiers right now is mobile apps. Consider these astounding statistics compiled in May of 2015:

- Mobile apps account for 52 percent of all time spent on digital media.
- Smartphone users spend 89 percent of their mobile media time using apps.
- 42 percent of all mobile sales generated by the leading 500 merchants came from mobile apps.
- Between 2004 and 2014, the average time people spent on their apps increased by 21 percent.
- 85 percent of people prefer native mobile apps to mobile websites.[8]

Clearly, apps are here to stay, and their number and popularity will continue to skyrocket.

Building an app to monetize for yourself is speculative. What I'm referring to here is charging business owners to build apps for them. Currently, there are about 19 million local businesses in the U.S. and less than 1 percent of them have an app, so there's huge opportunity in this space right now. Mobile apps are to small business what a website was in 2000 — the market is tiny but exploding as business owners are realizing how apps can help them.

You may not know how to build an app yourself, but you can outsource the tech work to a team of freelancers. Your job is to sell the app to business owners, which you can do via social media promotion. Your customers could be lawyers, real estate agents, chiropractors, dentists, doctors, restaurants, travel agents, nightclubs — virtually any business. Apps can help business owners market to their customers via push notifications, setting up appointments, featuring their Facebook and other social media pages, sharing YouTube videos, and more.

App-building software programs for less than $300 are making the process even simpler and cheaper. You could charge business owners an up-front fee of $997 for building the app for their business and apply a recurring $97 per month maintenance fee, while outsourcing all the tech work.

Coaching

You can create coaching programs for anything in your area of expertise and for which there is market demand. For example, you could coach people on fitness, public speaking, media relations, writing, visual or performance art, and even things such as fashion and appearance. *Fortune* magazine reports that it's possible to earn $50,000 a year coaching people to play video games![9]

In this industry as in others, technology is making it easier than ever before. You can offer coaching services via Skype and webinars and use advanced scheduling software to manage your calendar.

Consulting

Forbes reports that consulting is a $100 billion industry. The internet has broken down the barriers to setting up a home consultancy business. In most cases all you need is a laptop, cell phone, and the skills you already have with no investor capital. Consulting provides a great deal of flexibility, allowing you to set your own hours.

To become a consultant, you don't need a college degree, office, or staff. The overlap between your skills and the demand of the prevailing industry trends is your sweet spot. Take your existing knowledge and turn it into a resource that someone would be willing to pay money for.

A consultant is hired for one reason: knowledge. A client chooses you to work on her behalf because you know something that she doesn't. You help your clients solve problems and generate results for them. You get paid in direct proportion to the problems you solve.

Start with the base you have, either in the industry you're in now or one where you have valuable knowledge. Strengthen your resume with a strong track record of solving problems and being innovative with the company where you're employed. Build your credentials by creating a blog, writing articles, giving speeches, being active in professional organizations in your field, or publishing a book. Become known as an expert in your field.

Study your industry niche. Research popular social media posts and read the comments. Analyze the emotional and language level of the comments. Who are the top influencers in this niche, and what are they communicating to their tribe? Define your niche using buzzsumo.com. The tool validates how content performs online and breaks down that performance by multiple metrics across specific domains and keywords. This data assists marketers and consultants to better create, optimize, and promote their content.

One way to determine how much to charge for your consulting services is to find out what the competition's rates are. When ascertaining your monthly retainer, forget what it costs you and how much time each task consumes of your day. Focus on what the intrinsic value is worth to your clients. Determine the value of the problems you are solving for them. Companies are interested in revenue, so figure out how you can increase their profits.

When you start consulting while keeping your regular job, you may begin with one small project, then another. And then the client relationship can become ongoing. Building a consulting business can be tough, but it can be an opportunity to create income. It can become a bridge to exiting your regular job.

When you're starting out, use free social media platforms to build your prospective consulting base. Post on Facebook and offer your services to your community. Once you have secured two or three clients, you may want to consider paid social media advertising to scale up your consulting business. Freelancing as a consultant permits you to start saving money for investments and other opportunities to build wealth.

Social Media Marketing

Social media is a powerful way to market a business. Most business owners have very little knowledge of how to harness the power of the various social media platforms to generate new leads and customers. More customers for businesses will solve most of their problems.

If you are able to generate leads for business owners via social media marketing, you can write your own ticket. You can charge $1,000 to $5,000 per month per customer to manage their social media.

E-Commerce

Online entrepreneurs can generate income-building e-commerce stores on platforms like Shopify. A Shopify store can be filled with hundreds of products that can be drop-shipped from vendors directly to consumers. You can also incorporate targeted traffic generated from paid online ads on Facebook and Instagram.

The three essential parts of launching your e-commerce business include building the store, choosing your product niche, and finding product suppliers. When it comes to building your online store, Shopify allows you to rent a pre-built store and maintain it for less than $30 per month.

To best define your product niche and its commercial viability and market demand, use Google Trends. Go to trends.google .com, enter each product idea, and view the market metrics. When choosing products for your Shopify store, avoid products with prices more than $50. Cheaper products require less thought on the part of consumers.

When adding products to your store, the ideal solution is to source them through a drop-shipping service such as

AliExpress.com. You simply copy the product from AliExpress to your store, set your own retail prices, and after you sell a product, you purchase it from AliExpress and have it shipped directly to your customer who just made the purchase. To import drop-shipped products directly into your commerce store, you may want to use Oberlo.com. It is built for Shopify and specifically designed to manage your AliExpress drop shipping, and you can import hundreds of products to your store in minutes.

One of the benefits of building a profitable online e-commerce store is the ability to flip it for profit. There are astute online investors who have money to invest into profitable pre-existing stores that have been operating for at least two years. This unique opportunity for entrepreneurs enables them to build and flip stores in specific niches, maintain healthy profit margins, and implement a structured system with a procedures manual for the purchaser of the store.

When selling an e-commerce store, a business formula known as the earnings multiplier is used. For example, assuming the net profit after expenses is $7,000/month, or $84,000 annually, savvy investors may be willing to pay three to five times those net annual earnings to purchase the online store and its entire operational assets. This would make for a potential sale of $252,000 to $420,000.

Fix and Flip

By fix and flip I'm not just referring to real estate. I mean this in a larger sense of value-added reselling, meaning to purchase something at a low price that you can put some work into and then resell at a higher price. This can include real estate, cars, furniture, virtual real estate such as web domains and monetized websites, and more.

Some tips to consider:

• The bigger and more expensive the item, the greater the potential profits. However, this also makes for more up-front capital, more complexity, and greater potential for loss. For example, real estate gives you the greatest profit potential, but it also comes with the greatest complexity and risk, particularly if you've never done it before and don't know what you're doing.

- It's better to start small and then build big. The less you spend to purchase your first item, the less you have to lose if you don't make your money back. Start with something small, and learn the process as you build.

I started out with real estate in my teens doing fix and flip, but I quickly realized that it could easily turn into a never-ending hamster wheel. So while fix and flip can be used successfully, I caution you against seeing it as a long-term strategy. Ultimately, you have to convert your gains into cash flow. By continually selling your assets you forfeit the ability to generate ongoing cash flow. However, it may be an appropriate strategy for a short time in order to free up discretionary funds for investing.

I prefer to use the term "valufacturing," which I coined to give a more holistic understanding of fix and flip. It combines value and manufacturing, and means to manufacture value. With valufacturing, I look at underperforming real estate and businesses and see how I can add value to increase long-term profits. I'm not just looking for a quick flip; I'm looking for long-term cash flow and a potentially lucrative exit strategy down the road. The profit has to be in the purchase. My point is to not get stuck in fix-and-flip mode forever. Remember, ongoing cash flow is the name of the game.

Real Life Story

Derick Van Ness was able to build an automated cash flow business doing fix and flips. He graduated from college and started working a sales job in Los Angeles. After a few years, he got tired of working so hard for such little money. He stayed home from work one day to research other opportunities. Since his father is a contractor, he always liked the idea of fixing and flipping real estate. Derick thought, "I could buy a house, live in it, fix it up for $10,000 to $20,000, and then resell it and make $20,000. Three of those per year would amount to the same as I'm currently making, where I'm busting my butt twelve hours a day doing 200 cold calls a day."

So he started researching and came across a coaching program for real estate fix and flips. He purchased the course for $1,500 on a credit card, which was a lot of money for him at the time. The course proved to be a great investment. Derick found a new job that would give him more free time to work on real estate. He applied for more credit cards and, as he says, "basically stopped doing anything fun for about six months. For six months I just saved every penny I could." In the meantime, he was advertising to distressed homeowners.

Derick ultimately saved about $15,000 and had about $30,000 in available credit. When he started getting regular calls from people interested in selling their houses, he quit his job in July 2002. He remembers, "Two months after quitting my job I still hadn't bought a deal yet and I was spending money, so I was scared to death. I thought, 'What have I done?' But I just decided that I had already taken the leap and that I was going to ride this ship all the way to the bottom of the ocean, if that's what it took."

A few days later he got a phone call that resulted in his first deal. He put $500 down and took over the homeowner's loan. He quickly fixed up the house and sold it for a $17,000 profit.

Derick immediately began looking for another deal. Then he realized that he didn't want to do just one property at a time and that he needed more education. So he joined a local real estate club and sought out mentors. The president of the local club had a lot of experience, and she agreed to mentor him. With her guidance, he purchased two more properties. Within six months Derick had finished three deals and made about $50,000.

He started doing lots of automated marketing, which generated a number of leads for him, resulting in almost a deal a month for the next year. After making about $128,000 that first year, he decided to step things up. He paid $12,000 to another mentor and learned how to get even more creative with his deals. He reports, "There was a lot of value in having knowledge that other people didn't have, especially on the creative real estate side. Because a lot of my deals were predicated on my ability to create a transaction that maybe other people couldn't have figured out. By listening to the needs of the people I was serving and finding solutions that would meet those needs that the average investor probably wouldn't have figured out. That gave me a real competitive edge."

His other edge was learning how to generate deals through online marketing. He went from doing about one house per month to two houses per month. He spent a lot of time working on systems to make the process duplicable. He created templates for his contractors to use regarding the materials, making it easy for him to estimate repair costs.

He adds, "That really allowed me to automate the business to the point where I had an assistant in the office who prescreened all of my email and handled all of the incoming phone calls and paperwork. I also hired a salesman to call back on leads and put deals under contract. After about three years, I had the business to the point where, for the most part, I didn't have to show up to work." Derick's primary focus was on building relationships with people who could help him find deals or money. Then he focused on supervising his team. He ran the business until 2008 and ended up doing almost 150 fix-and-flip deals. He never even visited the job sites of a third of the deals he made. At that point, he became more passionate about coaching people to do what he had done, so he transitioned his business to coaching.

Domain Trading

The mad gold-rush scramble for buying premium domain names continues unabated with the evolution of the internet. Domains are a unique investment and can be acquired for as little as $10.

They are virtual real estate and limited in number. As demand increases, so will their value. Top-tier domains, particularly .com, .net, and .org, are considered the most valuable. Domain traders have been generating millions from domain trading since the 1990s.

You want to capitalize on trends and the mainstream newsfeed. Identify keywords that have a strong search engine ranking when considering any potential domain purchase. You can also take advantage of expired and misspelled domains.

One-word domains currently have the highest value due to their extreme scarcity. Two-word domains are my preferred choice now, as they offer the best investment value. The brandability of a two-word domain is exceptional. When choosing a two-word domain, does it roll off the tongue? Is it a catchy phrase, and does it make sense? Does it have search volume and high cost-per-click? When it comes to age, the older the domain name the more valuable it is.

Other domain extensions such as .rocks, .MBA, .sucks, .technology, and .earth are currently hot domain properties. (I personally own quite a few of the .MBA domains.)

Here is a short list of the most expensive domains purchased:

- VacationRentals.com: $35 million
- PrivateJet.com: $30 million
- Insure.com: $16 million
- Sex.com: $14 million
- Hotels.com: $11 million
- Business.com: $7.5 million
- FB.com: purchased by Facebook for $8.5 million

You can sell your domains by listing them on marketplaces. You can either set a fixed domain value or you can start an auction to lure higher bidders. Platforms such as hugedomains.com, auctions.godaddy.com, and sedo.com are marketplaces where you can buy and sell domains.

A client of mine has been investing in key domains over the past several years. He attended my master class six years ago and chose domains as his investment choice due to their low-price entry. To date, he has invested about $800. He just had his portfolio valued at $2 million.

To add more value to the process, don't just buy a domain and sit on it and hope someone will eventually want it. Take it to the next step. In addition to the domain, also secure social media profiles that match the domain. Then, build out a simple branded website on the domain. Essentially, you are creating and selling pre-built brands and assets to business owners.

The Sharing Economy

Also referred to as collaborative consumption, the sharing economy is based on people sharing their access to goods and services, and coordinating this sharing via community-based online services. In this new model, people rent beds, cars, boats, and other assets directly from each other instead of owning things themselves or purchasing them from traditional retailers and service companies. Just as Amazon allows anyone to become a retailer, sharing services lets people act as a taxi service or hotel. At the time of this writing, the consumer peer-to-peer rental market is valued at $26 billion.[10]

Harvard Business Review argues that the term "sharing economy" is a misnomer and that a more accurate term for it is "access economy."[11] We won't split hairs. The point we want to make is that this new technology-facilitated model is a great, simple way to leverage your existing assets to earn extra money on the side.

Here are just a few examples of ways you can use the sharing economy to boost your income:

Airbnb

Airbnb, VRBO, and other companies allow you to rent a room or your whole home to travelers, thus earning supplemental income with existing assets. In just over seven years, Airbnb has become a multibillion dollar company with more than two million listings across 190-plus countries. There are many things to consider before starting an Airbnb service, including municipal laws (many cities don't allow it); competing rates in your area; and the costs of hosting, such as cleaning, higher utility bills, taxes, and Airbnb's payment processing fee (6 to 12 percent). Your listing will be displayed on Airbnb's website, and you can also cross-promote it using any free social media platforms or your own website.

Airbnb arbitrage is the process of renting out a property that you do not own but rent for yourself. An arbitrage opportunity exists where you generate more money renting out the property on Airbnb than it costs you to rent from the landlord, providing you free rental status. If you want to rent on Airbnb, but have a landlord, approach him or her and get permission to rent out the space. Offer your landlord something on the income side, perhaps a flat rate or a percentage of all Airbnb earnings on the property.

One of Garrett's clients, Demi, was a single mom and yoga instructor. She heard about Airbnb and started renting out two bedrooms in her personal residence. She generated enough cash flow from those bedrooms that she was able to buy another home, move out, and then rent out the whole house. She now earns between $1,000 and $1,800 a month from her Airbnb property.

Uber/Lyft

You can earn money on your schedule. You give rides when you want and earn as much as you want, with the potential to make great money. Thirty hours of driving per week can generate up to $1,000 on average. You get paid weekly and your fares are automatically deposited. Additionally, this is a unique way to monetize your car, especially if you have a car loan. You could buy a new car and pay it off as an Uber or Lyft driver.

In late 2016, I was visiting London to deliver a keynote address. I had an Uber driver pick me up, and we struck up a conversation. He was a refugee from Afghanistan. He was generating $6,000 U.S. per month as an Uber driver. I asked him if he owned the Toyota Prius he was driving. He said, "No."

I dug deeper and learned that he and nineteen of his other refugee friends, who had all arrived within the previous four months, were all Uber drivers. They were renting their cars from another Afghan refugee named Akram, who had come to London four years earlier. These twenty Afghan drivers arrived in London with no money to buy a car. Yet now they're each generating an average $4,000 per month net after all costs.

Akram financed the cars and payed an average of $24,000 for each car. He rents them out at $1,800 per month each, which generates $36,000 per month ($432,000 per year) in revenues on twenty cars. He pays for all registration, insurance, maintenance, and fuel costs. The drivers simply spend their time and drive, and generate about $4,000 per month net after their rental fee. For these drivers, $7,000 can support their families for an entire year back in Afghanistan. Akram's plan is to upgrade his fleet to fifty cars. There are thirty other refugees on the waiting list to take up his offer.

And even if you don't want to drive for Uber or Lyft, you can still make money with them. There are plenty of people who have a driver's license but don't own a car. If you have an under-utilized car that's just sitting in your garage and depreciating in value, you can rent it out to ridesharing drivers. You can now list your car on HyreCar.com. An average car owner has the potential to generate up to $12,000 per year, providing a good source of passive income. Also, your car is protected under HyreCar's industry ridesharing insurance.

Poshmark

People buy or sell their clothing via Poshmark's mobile app. The premise is that you can "make money from clothes that are just sitting in your closet."

Fon

Fon enables people to share their home Wi-Fi network in exchange for getting free Wi-Fi from other users in the network.

TaskRabbit and Zaarly

Mobile marketplaces such as TaskRabbit and Zaarly allow you to hire people to do jobs and tasks, from delivery to handyman to office help. You can use these platforms to market your own services, from home repairs to iPhone repairs.

DogVacay

DogVacay connects dog owners with hosts who will take care of their dogs while they are away. Love dogs? Become a host and earn some money doing something you love.

Spinlister

Spinlister allows you to rent things such as bikes, surfboards, canoes, or snowboards to or from neighbors.

Lending Club

Lending Club is a peer-to-peer network for lending and borrowing cash. It's cheaper than credit cards for borrowers and provides better interest rates than savings accounts for investors.

Online Opportunities

There's no shortage of people promoting ways to make money online. Much of it is garbage, some of it is legitimate. Regardless of the scams and frivolous BS, the internet gives everyone unprecedented opportunity. For every way that currently exists for making money online, there are undoubtedly hundreds of ways that have yet to be created. It just takes some creativity, initiative, exploration, experimentation, and determination.

So much has been written about online opportunities that I won't belabor it here with tons of details. You can do your own research. My purpose is to simply give you some general ideas and categories that you can then explore more deeply. Consider these common and proven strategies:

Sell Stuff

Find stuff that sells, and list it on websites such as eBay, Craigslist, or Amazon. With drop shipping, you can open an online retail shop without purchasing inventory up front or managing inventory in a warehouse. You can facilitate all e-commerce products to resell using the Amazon or eBay marketplace. Using wholesale distributors, you choose the products you want to sell, add them to an inventory list, and then list them for sale. When they sell, you purchase the item from the wholesale distributor and have them ship it directly to the customer. You collect money from the buyer, and from your profits you pay back the wholesale distributor. In this model, the retailer never sees or handles the product, and doesn't deal with order fulfillment. As a retailer, your job is to find quality products and advertise them. Many drop shippers don't even need to have their own website.

The advantages of drop shipping are that less capital is required, it's easy to get started, overhead is low, you can work from anywhere with an internet connection, you can choose from a wide selection of products, and it's easy to scale. On the flip side, margins are usually low, and it's hard to keep track of inventory when you're not doing it yourself. There are also shipping complexities, and you often have to deal with supplier errors.

Real Life Story

Troy Remelski, one of the people mentioned in chapter 9, was an aerial acrobatics performer. After several years, the extreme physicality was taking a toll on his body, and he realized he'd have to find a new way to make a living. His biggest requirements were that he needed to be geographically independent and he didn't want to directly be trading his time for money.

Knowing he had six weeks before leaving to fulfill a cruise ship performance contract, he buckled down and researched ways to achieve his goal. By leveraging contract manufacturers and the Amazon.com selling platform, he knew he would be able to have someone else manufacture his product and use Amazon to warehouse it and sell it.

Armed with $1,000 from his savings and a few internet "how to" resources, he had a few hundred units of a product manufactured and shipped directly to Amazon's fulfillment warehouses. The first few sales slowly trickled in days before he left on his cruise contract.

Over the next several months he grew his business while he cruised on a ship off the coast of Antarctica and South America. Although hindered by the ship's poor internet speeds and paying for internet usage by the minute, he focused on his goal and reinvested his profits month after month. When his contract ended after seven months, he stepped off the ship knowing he'd never have to take another job again.

His business now generates millions of dollars of annual sales, and he runs it from a laptop or smartphone in just a few hours per week. Furthermore, he has leveraged the power of Cash Flow Insurance to aggressively save for his retirement, still knowing he can use that money in his business. He's able to borrow against his insurance policies to buy inventory in bulk quantities and pay back the loans through business cash flow.

Digital Information Products

Digital information products include e-books, training courses, software, website themes and plugins, and more. Creating products such as these is a way of monetizing your expertise in the form of intellectual property. You create a product one time, and then sell that same thing over and over again. You have no inventory, and you don't pay anything to duplicate each product.

As with anything, selling information products is much harder in practice than it sounds in theory. Not only do you need to know how to create something for which there is legitimate market demand and that will really sell, but you also have to know how to market it. You have to learn the various ways to drive traffic, from search engine optimization and pay-per-click advertising, to paid links and affiliates.

Revenue Subscriptions

A recurring revenue subscription is the holy grail of all business models and is indeed one of my favorites. I have several subscription memberships for people investing in the financial markets.

If you can sell something on a recurring revenue subscription, it gives you predictable cash flow because your customers are billed on a regular basis. It also allows you to manage the growth of your business. Recurring revenue is automated and creates brand loyalty as you deliver value to your customers every month. Every time your customer transacts with your brand, you're establishing more trust and forging a stronger relationship.

Netflix is the great example of a digital product sold as a recurring revenue. A much smaller company that uses a recurring revenue subscription is the Dollar Shave Club. For a flat monthly fee, subscribers to this service receive new razors in the mail once a month. If you have an existing business, bundle all your services into a monthly membership that your clients can subscribe to and bill them as a VIP monthly member.

Ad Revenues

You can make money by placing ads on a website, blog, or YouTube video. Honestly, this isn't easy to do. It takes thousands and even hundreds of thousands of page or video views to earn much at all. But it can be done, and lots of people are doing it.

Podcasting

A podcast is essentially your personal radio station. You record a show on a specific topic on a specific schedule, publish it via places like iTunes, and then market it to grow your listener base.

The Washington Post reports that the average number of podcast listeners has tripled to 75 million in the last five years.[12] Edison Research reports that 33 percent of people surveyed have listened to a podcast, up from 23 percent five years ago.[13]

As with any business, a successful and profitable podcast starts with defining your niche and providing valuable content.

Next, consider your format and content structure. You can do interviews or storytelling, you can share your personal thoughts or offer panel discussions. The average podcast length is usually between thirty and forty-five minutes.

Podcasts can be monetized through advertising sponsorships. Sponsors pay you a set amount per every thousand downloads or listens that your show generates. Once your podcast has become popular, you can create a suite of products to sell to your tribe of podcast subscribers. When it comes to broadcasting your podcast, you may want to include the podcast in your Google profile. Populate all your free social media profiles and feature links to your podcast. Include the show's notes or the main summary points. On Facebook, link to your podcast and include the show's notes in a status update.

Direct Sales/Network Marketing

Network marketing, or multilevel marketing (MLM), certainly isn't for everyone, but it can be a fantastic source of supplemental income, with the opportunity of becoming a very lucrative full-time income.

The major benefits of network marketing are the minimal up-front investment and the opportunity for leveraged income in the form of override commissions on everything sold by the people you recruit to your business. I would caution you that MLM isn't quite the passive income opportunity that at times it's sold to be. You have to stay in the trenches and keep expanding and motivating your team in order to build anything substantial. Still, it may be the right opportunity for you.

When you are researching a company that fits with your objectives, determine whether the company has a proven management team. What is the corporate track record? Has it built a billion-dollar organization? Are the products proven and are they affordable? What is the emotional context of the products? Do the distributors share the products because they love them and enjoy using them? Is there a proven training system with a strong focus on downline support and personal development? Is the compensation plan easily understood?

The anti-aging, beauty, wellness, travel, and lifestyle industries are the future of the MLM industry. The anti-aging and wellness market is a $3.4 trillion industry and three times larger than the worldwide pharmaceutical industry.[14] The booming lifestyle travel market is a $7.6 trillion industry,[15] eclipsing both.

MLM businesses are usually home-based, which allows you to set up a legal entity and take advantage of tax deductions.

Obviously, there are thousands of other ways to boost your income on the side. My goal here isn't to give you some exhaustive list of ideas, but rather to simply give you enough to get your creative juices flowing. I want to leave you with no excuses. In the history of the world, there has never been more opportunity than now.

Anyone in a developed country with determination can launch an entrepreneurial venture. You may not succeed right away, but if you stick with it, you'll learn what works and what doesn't. You can adjust with each new venture. You can make it happen. The only question is, how bad do you want it?

> "If you want something bad enough, you'll find a way. If not, you'll find an excuse."
> —NICKI KEOHOHOU

CHAPTER 14

ANALYZE INCOME OPPORTUNITIES

The challenge with opportunities isn't finding them; we're swimming in limitless opportunities every moment of every day. Rather, the challenge is knowing the right ones to pursue.

Initially, if you have little or no experience with entrepreneurship, your primary purpose is to simply get experience, as I did with guitar lessons and as Garrett did with auto detailing. Go implement an idea. Offer something to the world. Market and sell it. Learn what works and what doesn't. Learn how to adapt and grow.

This process is as much self-exploration as anything else. Along the way you'll learn what you enjoy and what you don't, what you're good at and where you need support. Your fears and blind spots will be revealed, and, if you persist, you'll learn how to deal with them.

Along the way you'll get more sophisticated about analyzing potential opportunities. First of all, consider the real value of any future business endeavor. Be sure to follow the money. Follow where the demand or main disruption is. You'll always be paid in direct proportion to the problem or service you solve. Make your money first, then pursue your passion. If your passion is underwater basket weaving or seventeenth-century wedding dresses, then your real passion is emotionally motivated and spiritually profitable, but lacking any fiscal logic because there is little monetary demand. Find the critical intersection of passion, skill, and consumer market demand. That's where the real magic happens.

Your Winning Ideas

Passion
what you love

Talent
what you are good at

Market Demand
what people will pay for

Passion alone won't bring you success in the field of your choice. People generally pay for skills, not for passion. If indeed there is market demand for your passion and it can be monetized, congratulations. Embrace it and enjoy the fulfillment it will bring. You now have a passionate career of choice. Passion is fuel, but it must fuel the right vehicle or opportunity.

The world is full of amazing, innovative, ingenious ideas that fulfill no real demand in the marketplace. The products and services that result from implementation of these ideas inevitably languish, because no one is willing to pay for them. Even if a product or service has a demand in the marketplace, the economics of fulfilling that demand might not make sense as a business proposition.

Even if an idea is well defined and promises to create a lucrative business when implemented in the marketplace, pursuing the idea further may be unwise if it does not engage your purpose.

Creation begins with an idea. An idea is turned into a concept. This concept is communicated to a team in a way that inspires their full commitment, and transforms the concept into an opportunity. This opportunity is tested in the market-

> "The future isn't a place that we're going to go, it's a place that you get to create."
>
> —NANCY DUARTE

place with only a small initial investment of input. If the marketplace is willing to pay for the idea's products, the systems for delivery of these products can then be perfected to achieve maximum efficiency.

There's a lot to consider when deciding which ideas are best to put into action. Making a good decision can save you a lot of time and resources. And the best choices can make the journey to your 5 Day Weekend faster.

After reading the Exploring Entrepreneurial Ideas chapter you probably have several new ideas. The ideas will continue to flow. Getting excited about your own business turns on the switch.

Garrett's Income Opportunities Score Sheet is a great resource for you to analyze your ideas. You can go to our website and download it to evaluate and score each idea.

Income Opportunity Score Sheet

Income Opportunity Idea _____

On a scale of 1 to 10, select the number that best describes your response to each question:

1. How much does the idea inspire you?
   (1 = No Passion, 10 = 100% Passion) ☐
2. What is the idea's potential for profitability? (1 = No ☐ Profit, 10 = Unlimited Wealth Creation Potential)
3. How many people would be impacted by the idea? ☐
   (1 = Very Few People, 10 = The Entire World)
4. Does this idea complement other areas of your business? ☐
   (1 = Limited Connection, 10 = Perfect Complement)
5. Can you delegate the work of implementing and ☐
   maintaining the idea? (1 = Must Do All Work Myself,
   10 = Can Delegate All Work)
6. Can you implement technologies to automate the idea? ☐
   (1 = No Automation Potential, 10 = Can Automate
   All Work)
7. Can the idea produce spinoff products and services? ☐
   (1 = No Potential for Spinoffs, 10 = Many, Easily
   Produced Spinoffs)
8. Does the idea fulfill your personal or business mission? ☐
   (1 = Goes Against My Personal/Business Mission,
   10 = Fulfills Personal/Business Mission)
9. Will the idea be profitable quickly? (1 = Profit May ☐
   Never Occur, 10 = Profit Occurs Before Any Expenses)
10. Do you have the capital (or ability to access the capital) ☐
    to implement this idea? (1 = Capital Not Available,
    10 = Idea Requires No Capital)

Total Score ☐

If your total score is less than 70, discard the idea. If your total score is between 70 and 85, examine more closely but don't spend much time or money. If you total score is greater than 85, move forward.

This score sheet can be downloaded at 5DayWeekend.com.
Code: P5

Garrett's team has developed a more comprehensive 48-point evaluation and planning tool called The Idea Optimizer. It's a system designed to 1) capture an idea, 2) define the process to create value in the marketplace, and 3) determine if the idea is worth implementing. To use it, just go to our website.

The Idea Optimizer can be downloaded at 5DayWeekend.com. **Code: P6**

> "Ideas are worth nothing unless executed. They are just a multiplier. Execution is worth millions."
> —STEVE JOBS

CHAPTER 15

BEFORE YOU QUIT YOUR JOB

Y ou're sick and tired of your job. Tired of someone else dictating how you spend your time. Tired of putting your passions on the back burner, of quietly surrendering your dreams. Tired of saying to your kids, "We can't afford that," or "No, we can't do that because I have to work."

You're anxious to get going. You can taste that freedom. You'd love more than anything to quit your job, like yesterday. I get it. But the first virtue you must cultivate on this path is patience. The 5 Day Weekend lifestyle isn't for the impulsive and foolhardy who rush headlong into things without thinking them through. It's a calculated, savvy, strategic approach to crafting a life of freedom. If you cannot currently work on your own dream, then temporarily work on somebody else's dream and learn from their mistakes.

Before you quit your job, there is a foundation to build. There are milestones to achieve and a mindset to cultivate. These include the following:

Milestones to Accomplish

Wealth Creation Account

The first milestone to achieve is to build your Wealth Creation Account. As mentioned in chapter 8, this is used to fund Cash Flow Insurance to take advantage of opportunities, as well as to serve as your peace of mind fund. Ideally, you want liquid funds totaling six months of salary. There may be exceptions. But it's important to have a safety net to fall back on.

Your peace of mind fund protects your mindset above all else. When you're stressed and anxious, wondering if you'll be able to pay bills on time, you're not able to produce at optimal levels. Your anxiety will get in the way of clear thinking and force you to make stupid decisions.

You want to be in a place where your decisions are not dictated by the tyranny of money, but rather by the goals you have set for yourself. You don't want to make decisions under duress, but rather when you are calm, peaceful, and confident. You're much more likely to make better decisions in that state.

Your Wealth Creation Account also allows for short-term capitalization on opportunities. You may find an opportunity for which you need quick cash that can be paid back quickly. This would be an appropriate use of this fund. This fund can also be useful for getting better interest rates on loans.

Six Months of Salary Earnings

My advice is that, in addition to building your Wealth Creation Account, you don't quit your job until your combined entrepreneurial income has equaled your job salary for six consecutive months. At that point, you've proven that you can replace your income without stressing. (And by hustling in your entrepreneurial ventures, you'll be able to build your Wealth Creation Account faster.)

The Mindset to Cultivate

Self-Employed vs. Business Owner

A lot of people call themselves "business owners," when in fact they are simply self-employed. They don't own a business — they own a job. They have no leverage. They have to do all the work. There's certainly nothing intrinsically wrong with this. The problem is that it keeps you stuck. You'll never achieve true financial independence as a self-employed professional with no leverage — and certainly no 5 Day Weekend.

I'm inviting you to think about this from a different perspective — that of true business ownership. Your freedom is a direct function of your leverage. The greater the leverage you have, the more freedom you have, and vice versa. The business needs legs beyond the owner. You build a business around your life, not a life around your business.

Active vs. Passive Income

You may not have instant leverage initially when you start your entrepreneurial ventures. It may take time to develop. But when you start a new business, keep in mind that the ultimate goal is leverage and passive income. Ask yourself this question about any venture: Can this be converted to a passive source of revenue over time? This may mean hiring other people to perform your essential functions. Or it may include leveraging technology systems.

If the answer to that question is no, it doesn't necessarily mean that you don't pursue your entrepreneurial idea. Sometimes, the right thing is just to do something to increase your income for a while. The increased discretionary income can then be used to fund something of a more leveraged and passive nature.

The point is this: Don't leap from the frying pan into the fire by quitting your job and building a self-employed position where you simply own a new job. In that case, you may experience a little more freedom, a tad more leverage, but it will never take you to where you ultimately want to go.

Don't Get Paid by the Hour

An employee will never get paid what he or she is worth. It's impossible for you to liberate your finances as an employee. Additionally, it's almost unheard of to be promoted more than three times in the same company. Get paid based on the value you bring to the hour. This starts with shifting your mindset from thinking in terms of dollars per hour to value per hour.

Get Paid to Think

The ultimate position for a 5 Day Weekender is getting paid to think. This means you have to become an expert at delegating. Those who get paid to work, work for those who get paid to think. When you are paid to think, many strategies that appear to be active income can actually be converted to passive income.

Much of this chapter becomes relevant later in your journey. However, it's critical that you start with an understanding of the big picture, a vision of what you're building toward. Big life transitions like quitting your job can be hard and scary. But you can take the fear out of the process by mitigating the risk through gaining the right knowledge and by building the right infrastructure.

A Bridge Out

If you have a good relationship with your manager and the company is pleased with your work, a freelance job with your old company could be your first entrepreneurial work.

> **"Action conquers fear."**
> —PETER NIVIO ZARLENGA

Call to Action

Your Entrepreneurial Income Plan

What are your top three ideas for increasing your entrepreneurial income?

Use the Income Opportunity Score Sheet in chapter 14 to analyze your ideas.

Develop a specific plan for implementing your top-scoring ideas.

Milestones Before You Quit Your Day Job

Milestone #1: Peace of Mind Fund

What is your current monthly active income?

Multiply that number by six and write it down. This is how much you want in your liquid peace of mind fund.

What is your target date for having this amount in liquid savings?

Milestone #2: Six Consecutive Months of Salary Earnings

What is your target date for achieving the goal of earning enough entrepreneurial income to equal your job salary for six consecutive months?

Go to our website to download and print this worksheet at 5DayWeekend.com.
Code: P7

You've established a solid financial foundation. You've been working hard to increase your income. You've put together enough assets to start investing. It's now time to start leveraging your assets to grow your money and shift from active to more passive income streams.

First, you'll want to turn any of your entrepreneurial business ventures that you can into more passive revenue streams. When possible, you'll want to leverage other people, technology, or systems to replace you as the one doing the physical work.

Next, it's time to start investing your discretionary income into passive income sources. You'll start with Growth investments, which I define as safe, conservative, and cash-flowing. As your investment income grows, you'll be qualified to invest in Momentum investments, which have high upside potential but also a greater ability to lose. These investments pay out in large lump sums rather than providing ongoing cash flow. The proceeds are used to reinvest into cash-flowing projects and assets.

For your Growth and Momentum investments, you want to look for alternative investments that you won't hear about from traditional pundits. These aren't your typical mutual funds, stocks, and bonds—they're much better, as you'll learn. These are investments that the wealthy use but aren't widely advertised or promoted in the media.

CHAPTERS

- **Build Passive Cash Flow**

- **Real Estate Cash Flow**

- **Cash Flow Growth Investments**

- **Go Big — Momentum Investments**

- **Why Conventional Investments Fail**

- **Seasons of Investing**

- *Call to Action*
  Your Investing Plan

CHAPTER 16

BUILD PASSIVE CASHFLOW

A common parable is told about a village with a problem. There was no water unless it rained. To solve the problem, the village elders decided to solicit bids to have water delivered daily to the village. Two people volunteered, and the elders awarded the contract to both of them.

The first person, Ed, immediately bought two buckets and began running back and forth along the trail to the lake, which was a mile away. He began making money right away, but he worked terribly hard, waking before the rest of the villagers to run down to the lake for the morning haul.

The second man, Bill, disappeared and was not seen for months. Instead of buying buckets to compete with Ed, Bill had written a business plan, created a corporation, found four investors, employed a president to manage the work, and returned six months later with a construction crew. Within a year his team had built a large pipeline that connected the village to the lake.

Bill's pipeline delivered cleaner water than Ed's, and it supplied water twenty-four hours a day, seven days a week. Bill was also able to charge 75 percent less than Ed.

Of course, Ed ran ragged while Bill was able to enjoy life—making money even while he was on vacation.

So the question is: Are you hauling buckets or building pipelines?

You may have to haul buckets for a while by yourself. That's okay. But once you've proven market demand and are generating consistent revenues, it's time to start building pipelines. You build systems so that you can largely step away from the business while other people run the systems for you. You still manage the whole process, but you don't have to be physically present to get the work done.

Three Levels of Entrepreneurs

Level 1: Wantrepreneur

Wantrepreneurs have plenty of ideas, but rarely take massive action. They struggle to get anything off the ground. They keep lining up new and better ideas, but they don't follow through.

Level 2: Solopreneur

"By working faithfully eight hours a day, you may eventually get to be the boss and work twelve hours a day."
—ROBERT FROST

Solopreneurs invest in their education and start a business working for themselves. They take action but, unfortunately, they've created a job with active income, and the business is 100 percent reliant on them. They start generating money and their business is doing increasingly well. They suddenly realize they are victims of their own success and that the business owns *them*. They are ultimately the operator, in the trenches and stuck in their business. The business needs legs beyond them.

This includes a wide range of professions, such as doctors, dentists, lawyers, accountants, plumbers, and technicians.

Level 3: Liberated Entrepreneur

This is the highest level of entrepreneurship. This is where you experience the pinnacle level of fun, freedom, and fulfillment. You focus on elements of the business that you are most passionate about and outsource specific tasks to specialists within the company. The liberated entrepreneur is the musical conductor who gets paid to direct an ensemble pit of musicians (specialists) who are tasked with the running of the enterprise.

Transitioning from Solopreneur to Entrepreneur

The biggest casualties of self-employment are your time and your freedom to travel. Here's how you can escape the self-employment trap and build a business that can eventually generate passive income for you:

1. Build the Foundation

First, you want to be very clear on who you are, what you stand for, what you stand against, and what you really want to define your organization. Write down your non-negotiables and never allow anyone in your organization to stray from them.

2. Hire and Train the Right People

There's an informal debate in the business world between Michael Gerber, the author of *The E-Myth Revisited*, and Seth Godin, the author of *Linchpin*. Gerber says that building a business is all about systems. He teaches that you need to make your systems so simple that pretty much any warm body can perform them. Godin says it's all about finding the right people—what he calls indispensable "linchpins." Linchpins are proactive, responsible, and smart. They see needs and fill them. They're full of ideas for improving your organization.

My take is that any business needs both, but I side with Seth when it comes to hiring. You don't want to base your hiring solely on how cheaply you can get workers. You want the best and the brightest who can adapt to change and proactively improve your organization. You want people who think like trusted stewards of the business upon whom you can depend to make good decisions.

Inexperienced employees may cost less short-term because of lower wages, but long-term, they may end up costing you more in money and time. Employ specialists significantly more talented than you are for important tasks within the company. If you're the smartest person in your company, hire more talent immediately because you're losing money. In business you must hire people to solve problems. You need to amplify and double down on your strengths and outsource your weaknesses.

The way to find the right people is to first define the position you need filled. Identify the mindset, skills, and other qualifications that are required of the position, and then hire someone who has those qualifications. There are some things you hate doing in your business that other people will love. Hire those people, train them, and let them shine. Also, never forget to treat your team with the same level of respect and care as you give your customers—or even more. This creates loyalty and empowerment.

3. Document Your Processes

Processes are basically the actions necessary to complete a task. Processes are generally labor intensive. Organizing and documenting these processes helps to create structure and define overall task flow for those doing the work. You can support and fine-tune them with procedures and technology later, but first you have to get a basic framework in place. Subscribe to and incorporate intentional task management. Add deadlines for each task, together with personal rewards, further incentivizing the commitment to completion.

4. Fine-tune Your Processes

Once you have general processes in place and the right people to run them, you add automated procedures by leveraging technology in order to become more efficient.

Processes are the big-picture steps outlining how you want something to happen. Procedures utilize technology to support processes, eliminating human labor where possible, and therefore creating scale in your business. Processes are about outlining how to do the right things in the right way. Procedures are about doing those things as efficiently and cost-effectively as possible.

Once you've developed your processes and procedures, include them in an operations manual, which you can use to train and manage people.

5. Leverage Content with Technology

Content is a powerful tool for implementing education-based marketing, claiming authority in the marketplace for your business, and telling your business story. Here are a few ways to leverage content:

- Blog articles
- Videos
- Audio recordings
- Books
- E-books
- White papers
- Email newsletters
- Workbooks
- Customer Relationship Management (CRM) and online marketing automation software
- Email marketing software
- Educational and content curation websites
- Online landing/sales pages for lead capture
- Automated email sequences
- Social media

Content and technology are critical for personality-based businesses. They make people feel like they know you even if they've never met you in person. Dr. Oz is an excellent example of this. No one thinks Dr. Oz is going to perform their regular physical exam, but they'll trust his recommendations because of how he's utilized the media.

6. Let Go

The hardest part of freeing yourself up as an entrepreneur is simply letting go and trusting your people, processes, and procedures.

Psychologically, this can be difficult because initially you'll feel like you're not creating value. In truth, letting go and freeing yourself up allows you to create even more value. You have to learn the difference between maximizing control and maximizing value.

Value maximizers understand that they have to take more vacations away from the office and allow their people to become empowered and grow. They have to trust others. Too many professionals, by focusing on maximizing control, become mediocre at a lot of things instead of becoming amazing at one or two things. This leads to exhaustion and, in many cases, even becoming resentful of their profession.

> The hardest part of freeing yourself is letting go.

The caveat here is that it's a huge mistake to hand off too much control too fast. Don't get so eager to let go that you create chaos. Think of this as a relay race. You need a good transition process. You need to adapt and adjust to challenges that arise.

But whatever you do, never make the mistake of believing you can't build a business. You can. And by doing so, you'll create more value and have far more impact than you ever would have working hard in a self-imposed job.

From $5,000 to $2.3 Million in 27 Months

Rich Christiansen is a highly successful serial entrepreneur who has built over a dozen multimillion-dollar businesses and authored several books, including the business bestseller *The Zigzag Principle*. In 2001, before everyone was doing search engine optimization (SEO), Rich learned it and was using it in his own businesses with great success. People kept asking him to do SEO for them, but he resisted.

Finally, a business partner convinced Rich to start a SEO business with him. They started with $5,000, which they used to go visit potential clients in New York with whom Rich had relationships. The first company they met with was Warner Music. They showed them a presentation and walked out with a $30,000 retainer fee.

Initially, he and his partner were doing all the work themselves. As Rich told us, "In the very first stage of business, your first step is to get to profitability. That means you as the business owner being very involved and doing a lot of work to figure out what works and what doesn't." They started picking up more clients and established a great track record. Next, they started marketing aggressively and a flood of additional new clients came into the business.

They hired a few employees and taught them their system. Next, they documented their processes in detail. At that point, Rich says, "I became more of a cheerleader. My job was to encourage, help, educate, and make sure people were following the processes." As the business grew, they brought in managers. Within twenty-seven months, the company was generating over $2.3 million in gross annual revenues, at which point they sold it to a publicly traded company.

Rich explained his process:

> There are three critical steps to building a scalable business. First, drive to profitability. Once you hit profitability, it's vital that you change your momentum, because at that point, it's really easy to get stuck as the technician, where you're still doing all the work.
>
> Once you are profitable, you have to shift and become a cheerleader and manager, adding resources and processes. You build up your teams, processes, and systems. In this stage, what's more important than what you do is what you *don't* do. There's a lot of hiring that takes place, but it must be carefully coupled with value decision making.
>
> In the next phase, you start developing products that can scale. You want to hit a leverage point where

all the work you've done can become an asset that is working for you. In our case, we developed a bunch of coupon websites that were automated. By the time we sold that company, we had a collection of close to 100 of these websites that were generating nearly a million dollars a year of revenue, at about a 50 percent margin.

Each one of those stages requires dramatically different behavior. The first stage is about dogged determination and doing everything yourself. The second stage is learning to step away and build systems and hire people to run the systems. The third is analyzing ways to scale.

From Golden Handcuffs to Freedom

Jason West is a fourth-generation chiropractor. When he first started his practice, his goal was to "be busy." But he quickly realized that being profitable was much better than being busy. This led to his being profitable, but still busy. He was working Monday through Saturday for almost twelve hours a day, for a total of seventy-two hours per week. He told his wife one time, "I can send you anywhere you want on vacation, anywhere. I just can't go with you."

He told us, "I thought I was building the perfect system only to realize that I had this wonderful golden handcuff, that I really didn't have a business. I had a job where I was working for myself but it was all dependent on me to make it work, which isn't really a business."

He took a step back and began thinking of ways to engineer the business so it would serve his life, instead of his life serving the business. He started by working five days a week instead of six, and then went down to four. Next, he started looking at what he could delegate. He hired a business manager and brought in other doctors. He explained, "I started figuring out exactly what patients need my touch for. I asked, 'How can I make it so they're getting the services and also getting my knowledge?' I don't have to touch every single person to make it happen."

Within months, his practice went from earning $1.5 million a year to $3 million a year—while he was working 33 percent fewer hours. The key, Jason says, is that, "You have to invest in becoming a manager and a delegator just as much as you invest in becoming a professional. And that's a learned skill set."

Jason has continued developing this skill set to grow his business without it requiring his direct involvement. He went from one practice to seven, and he's currently working on acquiring an eighth. His net worth has escalated by four or five times. He said, "When you can auto-pilot things inside of your business and get it to repeat with true automation, you move from having a job into owning a true business. I love the freedom I have to come up with an idea, put someone in charge of it, then get out of their way. And now, I realize that I make more money working *on* the business than *in* the business."

What If Your Business Can't Be Scaled

If there's absolutely no way to scale your self-employed venture, you've built yourself a job. In this case, recognize that and move on as quickly as possible. Do it only as long as you need the income. Shift your income to passive revenue streams as quickly as possible. It may be a good option for you to sell your business. That way, walking away isn't a complete loss.

> My goal is to get you out of a job.

Moving from a job to being self-employed is definitely a step in the right direction. It gives you more autonomy and options, and boosts your skills and confidence. Just make sure you don't stay there.

> **"A comfort zone is a dangerous place."**
> —MARY LOU RETTON

CHAPTER 17

REAL ESTATE CASH FLOW

Imagine working hard, saving diligently, and planning wisely to buy your first real estate property. You do your research and learn everything you can about real estate investing. You get your down payment ready and your funding lined up. You find just the right property. You're nervous, yet excited, as you close on the property.

You work hard to get a renter in place, and finally the first rent check arrives in the mail. It covers your mortgage plus gives you a few hundred dollars extra. It's an amazing feeling! You still have more work to do, but you've started. It's no longer just theory —you're really in the game. You'll have bumps in the road and you'll make mistakes. But you'll learn from them and your portfolio will grow, as will your passive cash flow.

Cash Flow Is King

Cash flow is the number-one reason for real estate to be one of your top considerations for 5 Day Weekend investments. Your goal is to create enough cash flow in a few years to fuel your desired standard of living in perpetuity.

In addition to positive cash flow, here are other reasons to love real estate:

Bonus #1: Leverage

With real estate you get instant leverage by paying a small percentage of the total purchase price as a down payment and then controlling 100 percent of the asset. And, over time as you make monthly payments, you increase your leverage because of the declining mortgage balance. Leverage enables you to borrow more to fund new investments that produce more passive cash flow for your 5 Day Weekend.

Bonus #2: Building Assets Faster

Because of leveraging, the net worth of a real estate portfolio can be grown much faster than traditional investments.

Bonus #3: Natural Inflation Hedge

As inflation rises, real estate appreciates at a similar rate over the long run. And, you can raise your rents (and cash flow) over time to compensate for inflation.

Bonus #4: Increased Tax Advantages

Interest on real estate loans is tax deductible. You can defer paying capital gains taxes as you buy and sell real estate via the IRS tax code called a 1031 Exchange. Plus, there are several other deductible expenses that help lower your taxes and increase your cash flow.

Bonus #5: No Early Withdrawal Penalties

Unlike 401(k)s and IRAs, you don't have to wait until age 59½ to access and leverage your equity.

Bonus #6: No Penalties for "Insider Trading"

In the stock market you get penalized for using confidential information to your advantage. No such penalties exist for being on the inside track with real estate.

Building Your Real Estate Cash Flow Machine

Real estate gives you more leverage than most investment vehicles. When you do real estate investing the right way, you can leverage your way to financial freedom within five to ten years.

Here are the basic steps to building your real estate cash flow machine:

> One good real estate deal could be the catalyst that creates your 5 Day Weekend.

1. Get your funding in place. Develop a relationship with a bank. Know what it takes to purchase investment properties. Start saving for your down payment.
2. Learn all you can about real estate language and numbers. Become a pro on the various strategies, terms, opportunities, and pitfalls.
3. Build relationships with real estate agents and others in your area who can help you search for new properties.
4. Buy your first property.
5. Build your team. If you're doing fixer-uppers, you need people to do the work. If you're just going to rent the property, you may consider hiring a property management company.
6. Continue buying properties, using the leverage of your existing properties.
7. Make your income stream more passive. Don't do all the work yourself—hire experts to do the work for you. Otherwise, you're just creating another job for yourself.

During the early years you will need to put a lot of effort into research, buying, and managing your property. Once your rental cash flow, with your other streams of passive income, reaches what you need to maintain the lifestyle you want, then you can hire a property management company to take over the day-to-day management and free you to fully live your 5 Day Weekend.

Use Leveraging to Grow Your Portfolio

Unlike traditional retirement plans, where you have to continue contributing to your nest egg out of pocket, a real estate portfolio can leverage and multiply itself. Do whatever it takes to get your first property, and that property can multiply into a large portfolio—all without your coming up with more money out of your pocket to purchase additional properties. Each additional home is purchased from the equity growth of the previous homes.

Let's look at a couple of real examples. Here's a property I purchased in Indianapolis:

Duplex in Indianapolis, Indiana

Summary

Number of Units: 2

Building Square Feet: 2,164

Listing Price: $99,500

Appraisal Value: $103,000

Purchase Price: $80,000

Loan Amount: $64,000

Down Payment: $16,000

Closing Costs: $2,800

Cost per Square Foot: $38.26

Cost per Unit: $41,400

Monthly Rental per Unit: $625

Projected Gross Annual Income: $15,000

Operating Expenses: $5,306
  (Utilities, property taxes, insurance, maintenance)

Annual Mortgage Payment: $3,672

Total Expenses (Operating and Mortgage): $8,978

Annual Net Cash Flow: $4,897

Monthly Net Cash Flow: $408

Note: This is only a summary. Fix-up costs are not included. See a more detailed example on page 163.

Your first goal as an investor is to generate cash flow. Your second goal is to create capital growth, or equity appreciation. As your equity increases, you can borrow more to acquire more real estate.

So let's assume you've purchased a property like the one above. You have some equity, and you're generating great cash flow. Now you have two options:

1. Hold onto it forever and just keep the cash flow. As the equity increases over time, you can potentially leverage it to buy more properties by refinancing or getting a second mortgage. Or, you can just pay off the mortgage and enjoy the cash flow.

2. Within a few years, after the property has increased in value, you can sell it to cash out, and then use the cash to purchase another, bigger property.

Let's say you go with the second option, to leverage your first property to build your portfolio. We'll assume the market appreciates well, and after three years of enjoying several hundred dollars a month of positive cash flow, the property is now valued at $120,000. You owe about $60,000 on your mortgage, so you have about $60,000 of equity.

You sell the property and, after paying closing costs, you walk away with $50,000. And in the meantime, you've saved more money and you have an additional $20,000 cash. You leverage your cashed-out equity and your savings to purchase a deal like this one, which I purchased in Orlando:

Triplex in Orlando, Florida

Summary

Number of Units: 3

Building Square Feet: 2,379

Listing Price: $369,000

Appraisal Value: $350,000

Purchase Price: $310,000

Loan Amount (30 years @ 4%): $248,000

Down Payment: $62,000

Closing Costs: $10,850

Total Cost (Purchase price plus closing costs): $320,850

Cost per Square Foot: $134.87

Cost per Unit: $106,950

Monthly Rental per Unit: $1,250

Projected Gross Annual Income: $45,000

Operating Expenses: $10,500
(Utilities, property taxes, insurance, maintenance)

Annual Mortgage Payment: $17,759

Monthly Mortgage Payment: $1,479

Total Expenses: $28,259

Annual Net Cash Flow: $16,741

Monthly Net Cash Flow: $1,395

Note: This is only a summary. Fix-up costs are not included. Closing costs were paid out of pocket.

Congratulations! You've leveraged your first deal, of $408 per month cash flow, to create $1,395 per month! You don't have to stop. Continually leveraging into bigger and better properties makes real estate so compelling and lucrative.

It won't be long until you're ready to buy your third property. And, then your fourth. As you move toward your 5 Day Weekend, you'll be building your personal balance sheet with value assets. Cash flow is your priority, but assets that continue to appreciate over the long run are a wonderful by-product.

Buying Your First Property

I purchased my first property as a teenager, an apartment for $152,200. In addition to all the cash flow I've received over the years, the same apartment is currently valued at over $1.3 million. This building with four apartments was built in 1928 and is in an exclusive neighborhood in close proximity to prestigious private schools. Within a decade, I managed to acquire the entire building and others in the same cul-de-sac. It was from this experience that I learned the leverage power of multi-family units.

Research and Leverage Resources

For your first deal, take your time and do your research. Finding the right property is the single most important thing you can do to be successful in creating cash flow for your 5 Day Weekend. Do your homework and don't buy until you find a solid property below appraisal value with a strong return. Engage with real estate agents to help you find the deal. Join local investment groups and network with other investors. Spend time on the ground yourself looking for deals. Scour the classified section of your local newspaper. Search Craigslist, the Multiple Listing Service (MLS), and Loopnet. Drive a different way home from work every day to look for properties for sale.

The difference between an amateur investor and a professional is that the amateur is anxious to make a deal, while the professional is patient. Professionals wait for as long as it takes to find the right deal, then pounce.

I recommend that you start with multi-family units (duplexes, triplexes, fourplexes, and more). Interestingly, it's often easier to acquire an apartment complex than your own single-family home. With multi-family units, banks are looking less at you than they are at the deal itself. If the numbers make sense, they'll consider it. With a single-family home, if you lose your tenant, you lose 100 percent of the rent.

Another reason I like multi-family investments is that you can live in one unit and rent out the others. The rents should outweigh all costs so you live rent-free. If you intend to occupy one of the units, you can also get a residential mortgage loan. Because the down payment requirement is usually less for residential mortgages, you can save money and increase your leverage.

Once you find a potential deal, do your research well. Make sure you can generate a positive cash flow on rent. Perform a home inspection to check for major structural issues. Get your funding in place. You're going to be nervous when you write the check for the down payment, but few things are more exhilarating than closing a deal.

The best deals always come from people in distressed situations, such as people who need to move quickly or who are in a tight spot financially and don't want to miss payments and get dings on their credit. If you've lined up your financing, you should be able to move quickly and snatch up these deals quickly.

Understand that you don't have to purchase exclusively in your local area. There are great markets all over the country, and you want to find those markets where property values are low and rentals are in demand.

Find the Right Property

When making a purchase, you want to pay the lowest price for a property that will generate the strongest return on your invested cash. As a guide, you want to buy properties at a minimum of 15 percent below list price.

Finding the right property is the single most important thing you can do to be successful in creating cash flow for your 5 Day Weekend. Do your homework and don't purchase until you find a solid property below appraisal value with a strong return.

The more you pay for (and finance) a property, the higher your monthly mortgage payments—and most important, the less your cash flow. The better deal you get, the more equity you have and the more leverage you have to purchase more cash-producing properties. Another thing to keep in mind: The more cash you need to fix up a property, the longer it will take you to break even on the deal.

Use the "Cash Flow Filters"

So how can you find the right property? I've created three Cash Flow Filters as a quick and easy guide to help you narrow down your choices and find the best deals. Then you can make your negotiation and purchase with confidence.

Cash Flow Filters

Filter #1: The Big Picture

Timing and Market
Location
Price per Square Foot
Seller Motivation

Filter #2: Analyze the Numbers

Down Payment
Closing Costs
Utilities, Insurance, Maintenance
Property Taxes
Vacancy Rate
Management Fee

**Filter #3: Physical Inspection
& Offer**

Physical Inspection
Execute on Contract

Filter #1: The Big Picture
Timing and Market

Before even considering properties, consider the timing. Is now a good time to buy? Is the market you're considering in a recessionary period with low property values, or is it currently experiencing a boom? Based on trends, how do you anticipate the market to perform over the next five to ten years?

Next, analyze the market in which you want to buy, whether it's your local area or out of town. What are the property values, rental rates, and vacancy rates? Is the population growing or shrinking? Are rentals increasing or decreasing in demand? What's the job market like?

Location
Once you've found a property to analyze, the first thing to look at is location. What's the neighborhood like? Who lives there? What amenities are available? Is the property close to schools and shopping? Will it require a long commute to work? Is it on a busy street or a quiet one?

Price per Square Foot
The next big-picture consideration is the price per square foot. You should know the average price per square foot in that area. If a property is priced below the average, you can immediately tell whether it is worth looking at. Anything above or close to the average will most likely get screened out, unless there are other factors that make it worth it. Anything below the average is worth checking out.

As I mentioned, you should be buying at least 15 percent below list price. This can vary, depending on the market and what the overall economic cycle looks like. The point is to not overpay. If the property looks good, make a lowball offer that fits the research you've done (see the next filters). The number of days a property has been on the market can be an indicator whether or not a seller is ready to lower their price.

Seller Motivation
If the price per square foot looks good, try to learn the seller's motivation. If possible, speak to the seller directly, or his or her real estate agent.

This is important because the more motivated a seller is, the better deal you can negotiate. People in distressed situations, such as being behind on their payments or going through a divorce, are much more flexible on price. They need to get out fast, and if you can move fast, you can solve their problem and be compensated for it.

Filter #2: Analyze Cash Flow and ROI

When you have favorable answers to the big picture questions in Filter #1 you can crunch the numbers. Do your research and plug the numbers in the Cash Flow/ROI Worksheet on the next page. Costs can vary greatly from property to property and city to city. They can make a big difference in whether you make an offer. It will take some time to do the research but that will give you the information you need to make a decision based on facts — not estimates, hot tips, guesses, or emotions.

With the worksheet you can learn whether the property's cash flow is strong enough and your return on investment (ROI) is high enough. Keep computing the numbers on various properties until you find one that meets your criteria. This may take weeks, even months, but it's a difference maker.

Here's an example of a completed Cash Flow/ROI worksheet. I used the figures from the Indianapolis property I purchased some time ago. You can find this information on page 155.

For this worksheet, the closing costs were paid out of pocket and not financed with the loan. We assumed the property would have a 7.5% vacancy rate.

Online Calculator

There's an interactive version of this worksheet on our website. It makes it easy to quickly crunch your numbers. A blank worksheet is also available for you to download and print.

After you complete the worksheet you will have a realistic estimate of the amount of annual cash flow that you can expect from this property. You can determine whether or not you should make an offer. For the drive toward your 5 Day Weekend, high cash flow is what you need.

Profitability is important. A good index to use is the ROI. By doing the analysis for a piece of property, you can determine if the ROI meets the minimum standard of a good real estate investment. Ten percent is a good minimum standard for the return you should look for.

5 Day Weekend Indianapolis, Indiana Cash Flow and ROI Example	
Property Purchase Information	
Property Type:	Duplex
Location:	Indianapolis
Number of Units:	2
Building Square Feet:	2,164
Listing Price:	$99,500
Appraisal Value:	$103,000
Purchase Price:	$80,000
Mortgage Years:	30
Interest Rate:	4%
Loan Amount:	$64,000
Down Payment:	$16,000
Closing Costs (Paid at closing):	$2,800
Total Cost (Purchase Price plus Closing Costs):	$82,000
Monthly Mortgage Payment (Principal and Interest only):	$306
Cost per Square Foot:	$38.26
Cost per Unit:	$41,400
Income and Expenses	
Monthly Rental per Unit:	$625
Projected Gross Annual Income:	$15,000
Less 7.5% Vacancy Allowance Set Aside:	$1,125
Projected Net Annual Income:	$13,875
Annual Operating Expenses	
Utilities/Internet:	$1,500
Insurance:	$1,290
Property Taxes:	$1,116
Homeowner's Association Fees:	0
Maintenance (Yard and House Repairs):	$1,400
Total Operating Expenses:	$5,306

5 Day Weekend Indianapolis, Indiana Cash Flow and ROI Example (continued)	
Annual Mortgage Payment (Principle and Interest):	$3,672
Total Annual Expenses (Mortgage Principal, Interest, and Operating):	$8,978
Total Monthly Expenses:	$748
Cash Flow	
Annual Net Cash Flow:	$4,897
Monthly Net Cash Flow:	$408
Return on Investment (ROI)	
Self-Managed Annual Return on Investment %:	26.0%
Less 7.5% Property Management Fee:	$367
Outside-Managed Annual Return on Investment %:	24.1%
Fix-up Cost at 5% of Purchase Price:	$4,140
Number of months until breakeven from rental cash flow:	9.8
Fix-up Cost at 10% of Purchase Price:	$8,280
Number of months until breakeven from rental cash flow:	19.6

Go to our website for detailed information about the formulas in the Cash Flow/ROI worksheet. Real estate professionals use several methods to evaluate property. Since 5 Day Weekend is based on cash flow, we've structured the worksheet and the online calculator to focus on cash flow. The online calculator makes it quick and easy to determine a property's cash flow and your return on investment.
Code: P8

If the results are strong enough, you can proceed to make an offer—as long as your contract gives you a way out if the next filter, a physical inspection, reveals things you didn't know about the house.

Filter #3: Physical Inspection and Offer
Physical Inspection

If a deal is good, you don't want to wait. After doing the numbers, submit an offer quickly while leaving yourself a contingency clause in the contract, which allows you to back out if you need to without losing earnest money or exposing yourself to legal issues. Then, once you have the property under contract, perform a physical inspection to ensure there are no major issues that will increase your costs significantly. In most cases, I recommend paying for a home inspection.

If the inspection looks good, move forward and execute on the contract. If it reveals issues that will prevent you from profiting on the deal, back out of the contract.

I learned from painful experience in my early years of investing to do my due diligence. As a teenager, I purchased three properties. With those investments under my belt, I naively believed I was invincible. I was in a hurry to invest and found a deal on some waterfront property. I spoke with a real estate agent about it, who was very convincing. My plan was to build a cabin on it. I bought the property, sight unseen, for $16,500.

When I came to inspect the property four months later, I discovered that it was underwater. It was in a flood zone and was underwater for seven months out of the year. I could sell the property today for about $5,000, at a significant loss. But I've kept it all these years as a thorn in my side to constantly remind me to do my due diligence.

Fix-up Costs Before Renting

You will rarely buy a piece of property that you can begin renting exactly as it is. Most homes will require some fix-up costs.

Start with a detailed cleaning of the home, including cleaning the carpets (unless you're replacing them). This shouldn't cost more than a few hundred dollars.

Next, do basic cosmetic improvements that make a big difference in the appearance of the home. I only renovate visible items. The main ones are landscape, front door, new paint throughout, appliances, and kitchen and bathrooms (new vanities, counter-tops, light fixtures, etc.). Repairing invisible items will not add additional value to your property (unless you absolutely have to in order to sell the property).

If you purchase a property in bad shape, you may need to do some deeper remodeling, such as installing new plumbing, electrical, or a roof, or changing the layout.

I learned from one funny experience how adding bedrooms can increase your rent. One day a police officer arrived at my home to arrest me for allegedly operating an illegal brothel in one of my rental properties. I said I had no idea this was happening and asked the officer to follow up with my property management company.

The property managers had failed to screen the tenants. The tenants were, indeed, operating a brothel out of the house. They had gone so far as to add two additional bedrooms by building dividing walls. (Apparently, business was that good for them.)

I evicted the tenants and shut down the operation. What I had originally rented as a two-bedroom house now had four bed-rooms, which allowed me to increase the rent by an additional $600 per month. I learned a valuable lesson: You can get more rent if you can add more bedrooms when possible.

I recommend that you do analysis before you buy the prop-erty to determine how much cash you will need to get it ready to rent. To determine your net cash flow (after you've paid all expenses and the mortgage payment), you want to have an ap-proximate cost to figure your cash flow break-even point. For ex-ample, if you were to put an additional $3,000 into the property and your monthly cash flow is $500, you would break even after six months. Then all the subsequent net cash flow is all yours.

My rule is to never put more than 15 percent of the pur-chase price into a property for renovations. One of the common mistakes is to put too much cash into the property and extend your break-even point too far into the future. Investing more may increase the value of your property, but when you are work-ing toward your 5 Day Weekend your priority is cash flow. Your growing asset is a great side benefit.

On the other hand, it's not wise to have a slum landlord mentality and put the bare minimum into the property. That results in the lowest rental rates and lower property value.

Overcoming the Down Payment Hurdle

You may be thinking that rental property looks like a pretty good way to create cash flow. But coming up with a down payment can be a real barrier to real estate investing. You may be thinking, "Where in the world am I going to get enough money for a down payment?" Aside from waiting until you save enough money, here are a few ways to overcome this hurdle:

1. **Borrow from Family and Friends**
   Those closest to you may be able to add to your savings, putting you in a position to buy your first property.

2. **Borrow from Your Cash Flow Insurance**
   If you have created and funded your Cash Flow Insurance, as detailed in chapter 9, this can be another source.

3. **Borrow from Your Retirement Fund**
   There are ways you can borrow from a qualified plan such as a 401(k) that can add to your down payment savings. There are lots of regulations, so be careful to avoid penalties.

4. **Federal Government Assistance**
   The Federal Housing Administration (FHA) and Veterans Administration (VA) have programs to assist first-time buyers who purchase duplexes, triplexes, and quadplexes.
   Garrett purchased his first property at the age of nineteen using a Creating Housing Affordable Mortgage Program (CHAMP) loan. With this loan he bought a three-bedroom townhome. He lived in one room and rented out the other two.

5. **Owner Financing**
   Sometimes the seller is willing to finance the purchase and take a smaller down payment.

6. **Find a Partner**

   Pooling your money with a partner offers a way to get started. Plus, there's one more person to help research and manage the property. However, you must trust that person, and you must get your agreement in writing.

7. **Hard Money Lending**

   Hard money lenders are private individuals or small groups that lend money based on the property you are buying, and not on your creditworthiness. They take first position on the loan, meaning if you default, they get the property. Hard money loans cost much more than a normal mortgage, including high origination fees.

Real People Building Real Estate Wealth

Garrett and I have been helping people create wealth with real estate for many years. During this time we have come across many inspirational success stories.

Engineer Sees the Light

Dale had been working as an engineer for years when he realized he was just working for a paycheck and had no passive cash flow. He was maxing out his 401(k) contributions, but when he did the math and figured out how long it would take him to replace his income with retirement funds, he decided to start investing in real estate.

Not having ever done it, he immersed himself in real estate books and courses. In September of that same year, he purchased his first property, a triplex for $180,000. He continued buying multi-unit properties, primarily in his local area. He didn't do any fix-and-flips, since his goal was to invest for cash flow.

Within 362 days of starting to work on real estate, he owned six properties with a total of fourteen doors. He was generating enough positive cash flow to cover his expenses and replace his job salary. He then used his real estate to leverage himself into various other ventures. Currently, his income is seven times higher than what he was earning as an engineer.

Dabbling Investor Decides to Focus

Pete is an entrepreneur and speaker who has tried a lot of different types of investments. To use his word, he was "tinkering" with the stock market, oil investments, real estate, and a few other things. He wasn't focusing on any of them. After looking at all his investments and realizing that real estate was giving him the most passive cash flow, he and his wife decided to zero in on that.

They got their start in real estate when they bought a personal residence in Colorado Springs, Colorado. A few years later, they moved out, kept the house, and rented it out. They did the same thing on their next house—lived in it for a few years, then moved out and rented it. On this move, they moved into their dream home.

Over the next few years, they saved money from their business and purchased four more rental properties, giving them a total of six. In 2015, they started considering vacation rentals via websites like Airbnb and VRBO (Vacation Rental by Owner). They started renting out their own home for a week at a time. During the weeks it was rented out, they would travel as a family. They were able to get $6,500 per week from their home as a vacation rental. At that rate, it took only eight weeks out of the year to completely cover their mortgage.

Realizing how successful this was, they purchased another nice home in Colorado Springs and furnished it as if it were their primary residence. Now, they rent out both of those homes as vacation rentals, and bounce back and forth between them depending on which one is rented out.

With their two vacation rentals and six traditional rentals, they are currently about 70 percent of the way toward financial independence.

Reluctant Husband Listens to His Wife

Bob grew up being taught the standard advice: Get a good job, save money, invest it in the stock market, and eventually you'll be able to retire. His parents mostly rented and they didn't invest in real estate, so he had no frame of reference for real estate investing.

Bob worked for thirteen years in the printing industry. On the side, he and his wife, Holly, started building a network marketing business. He quit his job when their business income was triple that of his job income. They were putting all their excess cash into the stock market, just handing it over to their broker without knowing what was happening to it. But they weren't making any money in the market.

Holly had grown up watching her parents invest in real estate with great success. She urged Bob to follow their example. But he was reluctant. So she started doing some research on her own and found a for-sale-by-owner duplex that she wanted to buy. She told Bob, "If you won't back me and I don't do this, I'm afraid I'm going to regret it for the rest of my life. And you wouldn't want that, would you?"

Being the smart guy that he is, Bob agreed. They bought that duplex in 1996. They had a great experience with it, but his real epiphany came one year later when they sat down with their accountant. Bob remembers, "Our accountant explained to us the depreciation schedule for the duplex and the tax deductions we qualified for. I started doing the math and thought, 'Holy smokes, this is fantastic!' Not to mention that our experience dispelled all the myths surrounding being a landlord. We've had great tenants, and we hire professionals to manage any problems we have."

Bob and Holly no longer put money into the stock market. They've built dozens of businesses that have generated hundreds of millions in revenues. But they view real estate as their retirement and security. They now own eleven properties, a combination of single-family homes and duplexes, which are worth a total of $4.783 million and generate $18,500 per month in positive cash flow. Bob doesn't regret listening to his wife.

Tips from 27 Years of Real Estate Investing

Obviously, this book isn't an exhaustive treatise on real estate investing. My goal is to give you enough of a foundation so you can move forward with confidence. Of course, you'll need to learn what works for you, but the following tips represent what I think are the most important things you need to know to get started in real estate investing.

1. The Profit Is in the Purchase

When real estate is done right, you make money not when you sell, but when you buy. I only buy property that is under market value and that I can confidently buy and sell on the same day for a profit, if that was my intention. I also look for properties that I can improve to immediately increase their value. The profit has to be in the purchase. I'm either buying below-market-value property, or one that is poised for significant capital appreciation based on market data and demand.

> Don't fall in love with a property. Look at the cold, hard facts.

You never want to bank on long-term appreciation in real estate. If it happens, great. But if you're depending on that to turn a profit, you may be waiting a long time. Plus, with long-term appreciation, you're not really adding value to the property or to the economy. This means that you have little or no control over your profits.

2. Buy Multi-Unit Properties

Today I never purchase single-family homes—all my property investments are multi-family apartment buildings. They can be easier to purchase, they're less risky, and they generate greater cash flow than single-family properties.

Don't overcapitalize on the purchase of your own residence. Think about freeing up capital to acquire multi-family units to generate passive cash flow. You may eventually decide to rent what you live in and buy what you can rent out, potentially saving you thousands of dollars per year in home ownership costs.

3. Don't Be Impatient and/or Emotional

When would-be investors first start out, they find a deal that seems to work and they get really excited. With that excitement comes a scarcity mindset and fear of loss. They get anxious to buy the property because they're afraid they're going to lose it. In that impatient, emotional state, they don't analyze the numbers carefully enough. Or if they do, they make the decision emotionally and then try to rationalize the poor numbers. Savvy investors know that there are always plenty of deals to be had. They don't get emotionally attached to any one deal.

Don't make real estate investing emotional, and don't be in a hurry. Take your time. There is an abundance of opportunities. If one deal falls through, there are ten more to take its place. It's far better to wait six months for a good deal than to act now on a mediocre deal.

4. Buy in the Right Location

You've heard it a lot, and it really is true: In real estate, location is the key to profit. The value of any real estate property is driven by location and market demand. By location I'm referring both to the micro level of the particular neighborhood as well as the macro level of the city or region in which you buy. Study market trends to understand where the deals and demand are.

5. Find Properties in Which You Can Build Sweat Equity

Look for properties in which you can apply a little "sweat equity" toward some basic improvements. I don't purchase new properties. Why pay a hefty profit to a developer? There is zero value to be added. Always look for properties that you can valufacture.

6. Be Smart About Renovations

When I was starting out, it was all about sweat equity. I assembled a small crew of skilled workers to help me renovate my first purchases. I often worked side by side with them. Over a period of time, we developed a cookie-cutter system where every property looked exactly the same inside. We frequently used the same paint color, carpet, tiling, stone, wood floors, and cedar blinds for all properties.

The rules were clear. With every project we renovated the kitchen and bathrooms, which is where you can increase the value the most. First impressions count when walking up to the premises, so we always painted or replaced the front door. We added new grass and plants, as well as a nice mailbox at the curbside. These are enhancements that increase the value of the property.

With all renovations, I keep my budget expenses to no more than 15 percent of the purchase price. I allocate a percentage of my budget to the different elements that need work. Depending on the property, I may consider allocating 30 percent of the budgeted funds to the kitchen, 20 percent to the bathroom, 20 percent to the exterior, and 30 percent for general improvements.

If a property can't meet my budget criteria, I don't purchase it. The rule is to renovate for profit. View the valuation of comparable renovated properties in the area for further validation.

7. Add Value to Rent Out Properties Faster

All my rentals come with appliances, including a fridge, oven, dishwasher, and microwave. I include Wi-Fi and cable TV for free, but I add the cost of those into the rent. Adding such amenities allows me to rent out my properties faster.

8. Manage Your Property Wisely

A common way that inexperienced investors lose their shirts and get disenchanted with real estate is by not managing their investments properly. Amateurs who haven't done their research have no mechanism for collecting rent. They don't properly screen tenants and thus have to deal with bad ones. When tenants don't pay rent on time, inexperienced investors are too lenient because they don't want to be "mean."

Inexperienced property investors may also do a poor job of managing the finances. They may not take into account additional costs, such as taxes and vacancy, or have a large enough emergency fund to handle repairs and maintenance. They get so excited about the idea of passive income that they neglect the management of their properties. As a result, they have a bad experience and end up saying things like, "Real estate is a bad investment."

It's possible to properly manage your properties yourself if you know what you're doing and you want to spend the time it takes. For most people, I recommend using a property management company to make these real estate investments even more passive. The added fees are well worth the reduced hassle.

9. Have a Peace of Mind Fund

Make sure you have enough liquidity (cash on hand) to handle maintenance and repairs, bad tenants, or vacancies. As a rule of thumb, you should have at least six months of mortgage payments in a separate bank account.

Also, keep in mind that your Cash Flow Insurance policy is an excellent resource for this.

10. Hold onto Your Cash

Cash is precious because it's used to buy assets that convert your cash into cash flow. The more cash you sink into one property, the less you have for other deals.

You can make this mistake in a few ways. First, you can buy a property that is too expensive. The more expensive the property, the bigger your down payment. Also, with single-family investments, the more expensive the home, the greater the risk. If all of your cash is wrapped up in one property that doesn't have sufficient cash flow or isn't easy to sell, you're in trouble.

You can also make this mistake by putting too much money down, and by doing too short of a loan term, which makes for a high payment. *Always* opt for the lowest down payment possible and the longest loan term available. You want to stay as liquid as possible; money tied up in property equity may not be easily accessible.

11. Don't Over-Leverage

One strategy that wiped out many property speculators in the last financial crisis was borrowing 100 percent on properties. Banks were handing out loans like candy — and not just any loans, but crazy loans based on stated income, with no documentation or down payment required. As a result, inexperienced investors got over-leveraged, and when the market crashed they were upside down and in over their heads.

Buying when the market is high and borrowing 100 percent of the purchase price leaves you with no viable exit strategy — short of foreclosing, giving the property back to the bank, and killing your credit.

When you buy a property at least 15 percent below market value and put 20 percent down, you have a built-in buffer should the market crash. Furthermore, your rental cash flow should always exceed your mortgage payment regardless of what the market does. You build your exit strategy into your purchase, versus trying to figure it out when something bad happens that's out of your control.

Don't be afraid of borrowing, but respect it. It can be an amazing tool when leveraged wisely, but it can kill you when you overuse it.

12. Understand Market Volatility and Exit Strategies

It benefits you to understand how market shifts will impact your property. If the market tanks, will you still be able to cover the mortgage in rent? If you can't sell the property, can you still generate a positive cash flow?

You also want to know what strategies work best in which markets. For example, recessions are often perfect for rentals because a lot of people get credit dings and can't get financing, but they can still afford to pay rent.

Finally, what is your exit strategy? Do you plan on holding onto this property forever? Will you sell and purchase a better property, using a 1031 Exchange, if the property appreciates to a certain level? If you had to, would you be able to sell it quickly for a profit, or will you have to wait out the market? One of the worst-case scenarios in real estate investing is having a property that you can't sell and that is draining money month after month.

You Can Do This!

Real estate has been good to me over the past two-plus decades. In fact, it's been one of my primary strategies for creating my 5 Day Weekend. I know it can do the same for you.

Real estate isn't always easy. It can be hard and complicated. You can definitely make mistakes and lose money. But it's also worth it! Few things give you greater leverage and more investment advantages than real estate. You just have to stick with it. Research as much as you can. Take action. Learn from your mistakes, and keep moving forward.

In the end, when you're living your 5 Day Weekend, you'll be glad you did.

> "Landlords grow rich in their sleep without working, risking or economizing."
> —JOHN STUART MILL

CHAPTER 18

CASH FLOW GROWTH INVESTMENTS

In the Growth phase, your goal is to convert your income into more passive, cash-flowing income streams that are safe and conservative. Money that you use to fund your Growth investments has been generated from your hard-earned active income—your blood, sweat, and tears. You have an emotional attachment to that money, and for good reason. Never speculate with this money. Anything you do has to meet the following criteria:

1. You must understand the potential return on investment up front.
2. You must know how to manage and mitigate your risk up front. You must understand your worst-case scenario. Your

investment must have solid safeguards built in to drastically reduce your risk.

3. Your investment must be recession resistant. If you're relying on the market to go up, it's not recession resistant. If there's a good chance the value will drop in an economic downturn, determine how much and carefully evaluate.

4. You must be able to control the investment. Do you have an exit strategy? Do you have liquidity? Do you know how it works? Can you influence the outcome, or are you dependent on various factors beyond your control?

5. Geo-lifestyle optimization. You must be able to invest while maintaining a "travelpreneur" lifestyle. In other words, can you make the investment from anywhere in the world?

I teach people that the number-one secret to riches is to sell the pans, picks, and shovels during a gold rush. Always service speculation and exorbitant demand. While others are frantically speculating, you should operate from certainty and abundance. Prospectors in a gold rush are speculating with only the hope of making money. Investors know exactly how they're making money, and how to do it whether the market goes up or down.

In other words, think like a casino. Rig the game in your favor. Remember: You know the odds are stacked against you when you have no idea what your return on investment is up front. As an investor in the Growth phase, you make your profit on the investment up front when you buy.

Investment Strategy

There are two basic investment strategies. The following 5 Day Weekend Plan illustration shows the difference.

The conservative option (A) is to continue to use your Growth Investing income for lower-risk Growth Investing. You keep scaling up your passive income ratio (PIR) and passive income. This allows you to draw on this cash flow source for your Lifestyle Living. The amount you use for your lifestyle can increase as your passive/active ratio increases.

The aggressive option (B) is to add the higher risk, but greater payoff potential, Momentum Investing to your Growth Investing foundation. It's important if you choose the aggressive option that you continue to add to your Growth Investing foundation. You will continue to use your cash flow from Growth Investing to fund and service your Lifestyle Living.

Investment Income Flow

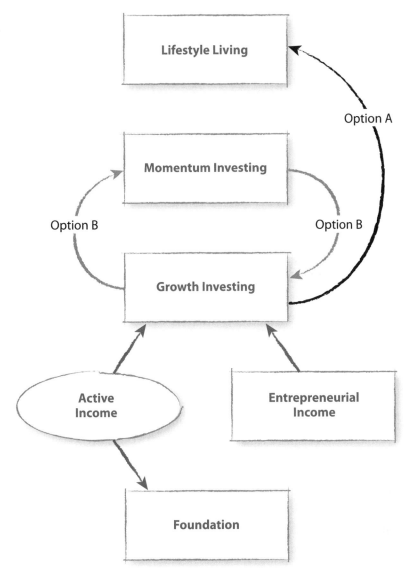

Growth Investment Opportunities

Below are a few Growth investments I've been using for decades to generate passive income. I call them "cash flow–optimized" investments because they're not what you'll typically hear about from mainstream financial media or what's being sold by conventional retirement planners who sell you products from which they make the highest commissions.

Also, understand that I provide these not as an exhaustive list, but rather to simply give you ideas of what's available. There are many other investments to consider as well. As a rule, when considering investments, think in terms of optimizing cash flow immediately versus accumulating for the long haul.

Tax Lien Certificates

Counties require property taxes to be paid so that they can fund the many public services offered to the community. Property taxes are a major source of revenue for counties. If property owners fail to pay their property taxes, then there is a financial shortfall of revenue for the county, which will have adverse effects on the community. When property owners become delinquent on their property taxes, the city or county in which the property is located can place a lien on the property.

A lien is a legal claim against the property for the unpaid amount that is owed. A property with a lien attached to it cannot be sold or refinanced until the taxes are paid and the lien is removed. A tax lien certificate is a first-position lien on real estate. In other words, it's the obligation to pay property taxes before any other debts are paid. A tax lien certificate is created by the municipality and reflects the amount that is owed on the property tax plus any interest penalties due. These certificates are auctioned off to investors. Tax liens can be purchased for as little as a few hundred dollars, and can be as high as hundreds of thousands of dollars. They can be purchased on residential or commercial properties, or undeveloped land. Investors buy them because property owners must pay off the lien with interest in order to remove the lien. That interest goes to the investors who have purchased the liens. In other words, tax liens come with legally mandated returns. They are among the safest and highest-yielding investments you can find for the small amounts needed to invest. They pay an annualized interest rate return from between 12 to 18 percent, even as high as 36 percent interest per year. Think of how much interest your savings bank is paying you right now. You don't have to settle for the measly returns financial institutions want to give you.

If a property owner fails to redeem and pay off their taxes, the investor can begin the foreclosure process and take the property. So you either earn a secured high interest rate or, by law, you own the property free and clear with no mortgage. If you do acquire the property, you end up owning the property for just the back property taxes, penalties, interest, and foreclosure costs. By acquiring properties this way, you may resell them at market value or keep and rent them out. Statistically, only a very small percentage of property owners are foreclosed on with tax certificate liens. Most liens tend to be redeemed by the owner.

Interest accrues on tax lien certificates on a monthly basis or a maximum percentage per year, counting each fraction of a month as an entire month, from the month of purchase. For example, suppose John purchases a tax lien certificate for $500 at a tax sale in Maricopa County, Arizona, with an interest rate of 16 percent. The property owner redeems on the lien, paying the county $500 (tax amount) plus $80 (penalty amount). The county then pays John his original investment of $500 plus $80 interest, for a 16 percent return.

Tax liens are a socially responsible vehicle. They actually help the property owners because they extend the amount of time needed for the owner to pay his taxes. The amount of time in which the property owner has to pay his taxes is known as the "redemption period." The redemption period can be anywhere between three months and four years and starts from the day of the tax sale.

Each year, up to $10 billion of tax liens are issued in the U.S. You'll have a regular supply of liens to invest in. You don't have to

Tax Lien Process

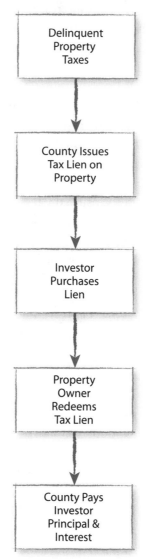

attend auctions in person to buy liens. More and more counties are making them available online, which means you can invest in them from anywhere around the globe as long as you have an internet connection. Check with the tax office in the county in which you are looking for property. It can provide information about that county's specific process.

Investing in tax lien certificates is recession and depression resistant. Property taxes must be paid regardless of what the economy is doing. During a recession, tax liens are actually more lucrative because there is a higher probability of acquiring valuable real estate for pennies on the dollar. Tax lien investing requires up-front capital and takes at least 120 days to see a return on your investment. The key is to research the property and know as much as you can about the neighborhood and county.

There are a few potential downsides of tax liens to be aware of, including the following:

- **Foreclosure Risks:** If the property is sold to pay off outstanding debt, you may not get your money back if other creditors have claims that take priority over yours. Check to see if there are any other liens against the home.
- **No Liquidity:** Once you buy a tax lien, your money is tied up. You can't ask for your cash back. You don't know how long it will take for the homeowner to pay off the tax lien.
- **Worthless Property:** If you buy a tax lien on a property that no one wants, the taxes may never be paid and your certificates will be worthless.

I should also note that tax lien investing is not technically passive, meaning you have to actively find, purchase, and manage liens. However, it can quite easily be turned into passive income by creating a team to do the work for you, as I've done. A number of years ago, I trained and delegated all tax lien investing to one of my outsourced assistants. Using strict criteria and a checklist, my assistant researches and secures liens on my behalf, and I pay her 10 percent of all profits generated. By delegating, I've turned what once was a three- to five-hour per month active income strategy into a completely passive stream of income for myself.

Glenda is a property investor who was in search of additional cash flow to service her property portfolio. She used the tax lien strategy taught by one of my training organizations. She made her first deal in less than thirty days and acquired five tax liens and two tax resale properties. She is earning 18 percent interest on the tax liens. In the past seven months, Glenda has generated a net income of $27,695.39. The best part about it is that she makes her investments from home or other parts of the world when she is traveling. She also has two properties valued at $128,000, which she purchased at 8 cents on the dollar. She said, "I wanted safety, I wanted consistency, and I wanted predictability, and that's exactly what I got with tax liens."

 For more information on tax lien investing, visit 5DayWeekend.com. **Code: P9**

Renting Out Shares on Wall Street

When it comes to the financial markets, I prefer a short-term strategic play where you're only exposed to the market between one to three weeks at a time. One investment method that I've personally used for more than two decades is the Sharelord Strategy.

Just as a landlord rents out an investment property to a tenant, the same strategy has existed within the stock market since 1973 when the Chicago Board Options Exchange opened. Investors can generate rental income by simply renting out their share portfolio to options traders on the options market. By renting out their shares, investors get paid either a weekly or monthly cash-flow rental based on the contract period of the options contracts they create.

The technical term for this strategy is "covered calls." To clarify any confusion and to best explain this strategy, I coined the term "Sharelord" a couple of decades ago. The words "shares" and "stocks" are used interchangeably, referring to stock certificates that denote ownership in a company.

As a Sharelord, we give the tenant, who is the call option buyer and speculator, the right but not the obligation to purchase our shares. Call option buyers choose to trade the contracts of our shares in lieu of purchasing the shares outright. They trade the options contract with the hope of selling it for a profit before the options contract expiration period.

As a Sharelord, we service this speculative buying demand by creating the market for it. Just like the gold rush days, a

Sharelord will sell the pans, picks, and shovels to speculators hoping to strike it rich. We are capitalizing on those who want to speculate and buy call options on shares. On Wall Street, 95 percent of speculators will trade the market and 5 percent will create it. As a Sharelord, we create and service speculative market demand.

For the right to purchase our shares, the speculative call option buyer—who is the tenant of our shares—buys a call option. We select the selling price of our shares, nominating a strike price, and collect the options premium from the call option we just created. In the event the options buyer exercises the right to buy our shares, we simply surrender our shares.

In options trading, the buyer of the call option contract may exercise the right to buy the underlying shares at the specified price. For call options, the strike price is the price at which the underlying stock can be purchased. Speculators are hoping that the market price of the stock exceeds the strike price.

If our shares are exercised, meaning the speculators buy them from us at the strike price, we can acquire new shares to rent out the following month. If our shares are not exercised, we re-rent out the same shares we own for a new contract time period.

Here's how it works: I purchase a minimum of one hundred shares of any particular stock. One hundred shares equal one contract. Let's say we purchased one hundred shares of XYZ stock at $8.80 (value = $880) and rented them out at the strike price of $10 for the month to a call option buyer. Assuming we received $0.44 per share ($44), this would equate to a 5 percent return. If our shares were exercised at the strike price of $10 by the call option buyer, we would receive $10 per share and our cash flow return for the month would skyrocket to 18.6 percent. This scenario offers us a second opportunity to generate additional cash flow.

As added protection, a Sharelord investor can purchase stock market insurance, otherwise known as a put option, while renting out their shares. This protects their share portfolio, thus providing further downside protection. By using a small portion of the rental premium that was generated from renting out the shares to purchase the insurance, the Sharelord investor is effectively using none of their own money.

Most shareholders today buy shares and hold them without generating any rental income. They buy with the hope of selling the shares at a higher price for profit. This is the equivalent to a property investor having investment properties and keeping them vacant, not realizing they could rent them out and generate an income. The only way they make money is if the share price rises — and they have zero control over that. They don't understand that they can actually write a call option on their shares and rent them out to generate cash flow whether the share price rises or not.

The share renting strategy is designed for share market investors who have been thinking about high-return strategies but don't know where to start, or those whose traditional forms of share ownership are not producing the returns they want. It's a perfect complement to real estate investing. The Sharelord investor strategy provides the cash flow to acquire more properties.

For more information on the Sharelord renting strategy, visit 5DayWeekend.com.
Code: P10

The "Bank Strategy"

Billionaire Warren Buffett is one of the world's wealthiest investors. His company, Berkshire Hathaway, is a heavy investor in the insurance industry, generating billions in premiums. Over the past decade, it has amassed a significant war chest of available cash flow reserves that have yet to be paid out to cover insurance claims in the future. Berkshire Hathaway has used these cash reserves to purchase and revitalize struggling businesses.

The lifeblood of Warren Buffett's cash flow system — insurance premiums — inspired my "Bank Strategy" well over a decade ago. The Bank Strategy is a term I coined, and it involves creating insurance policies to generate premiums using options credit spreads on the financial market. A credit spread involves simultaneously selling and purchasing an options contract in the same expiration month, but at different strike prices.

I create these credit spreads using the diversified portfolio of the S&P 500 index, which is a basket of the leading 500 stocks in the world. Creating credit spreads on the entire S&P 500 gives me more control and less market volatility.

Here's how it works. I create an insurance policy on the performance of the S&P 500. Speculators, traders, and hedge fund managers buy these insurance policies to hedge their bets. These contract buyers are "worried bulls," meaning they believe the market is going up, but they want to mitigate their risk. If the market goes up, they're only out the relatively low amount they've paid for the insurance policy. If the market declines significantly and they lose money, the insurance policy pays out to restore what they lost.

Insurance companies mathematically stack the odds in their favor; only a small fraction of policyholders ever make a claim on their insurance, and the insurance companies keep the majority of the premiums paid. Research shows that most options contracts in the financial markets expire worthless and without claim. A Chicago Mercantile Exchange study of all S&P 500 options found that 93.9 percent of them expired worthless.[16] With the Bank Strategy, we apply the same mathematical methodology. I incorporate the Bank Strategy as a form of cash flow to be used for purchasing property assets and other investments.

Traditional insurance policies underwritten by insurance companies have expiration dates of up to twelve months. With the Bank Strategy, we create the insurance contracts in the financial markets with a lifespan of just seven days, minimizing our risk and time in the market. We identify a "safe zone" and create an insurance policy contract at a certain price below the current pricing action of the S&P 500 each Friday. Then we close out the insurance contracts the following week on Thursday. So long as the S&P 500 trades above our "safe zone," we remain in profit. The entire S&P 500 index would have to seriously plummet for there to be any risk to our positions.

I personally transact the Bank Strategy every week of the year, and it takes less than one minute each Friday. Each Friday I inform my broker via text or email about how many insurance contracts I want transacted. The objective is to bank weekly cash flow from the premiums we receive and profit from the leading 500 companies of the index.

This lazy "money game" strategy, with its mathematical probability (if played correctly), has serious appeal. In a free market economy, there are no borders or restrictions as to how much money anyone can generate. Your ethnicity, your level of education, or your IQ is irrelevant when it comes to generating it.

Joel was a beginner investor who didn't know where or how to start. He had aspirations to reduce the hours he worked in construction and complained about never experiencing any kind of investment success. He was looking for a passive, low-risk/high-return investment that worked whether the financial markets moved up, down, or sideways. He started with the Bank Strategy, doing several insurance contracts each Friday. Within six months, he scaled this to over sixty-eight contracts each Friday, generating him $47,896 in net income. Joel says, "The Bank Strategy beats doing construction all day every day." Joel wants to potentially leave his day job in the next three years. He wants the Bank Strategy to boost his cash flow reserves to pursue travel plans and his passions in life.

 For more information on the Bank Strategy, visit 5DayWeekend.com.
Code: P11

Storage Units

Every year Americans spend billions of dollars on electronics, clothes, toys, and household items. The average home in the U.S. has nearly tripled in size over the past 50 years. In this consumer-driven economy one out of every 10 Americans rents a storage unit. This represents the fastest growing segment of the commercial real estate industry.

Building or buying storage units is another excellent way to leverage real estate to generate cash flow. You receive cash flow from rent, and if tenants don't pay you can auction their stuff and evict them. They require a lot of money up front, but it's hard to beat the cash flow you can get from them. Recessions also create more demand for storage units. People unfortunately lose their homes and require storage unit capacity to store their belongings.

Before investing in storage units, consider these points:

- **Geography:** Make sure you're not building or buying in an area where there's an oversupply of self-storage options.
- **Location:** Are there competitors nearby? Does the location have good visibility?
- **Management:** With storage units, you're not just buying a piece of real estate. You're buying a business that needs to be managed properly. Make sure you hire the right staff and give them adequate training and systems.
- **Maintenance:** If you're buying existing units, inspect them for maintenance issues like leaky roofs or mold. Make sure you provide proper maintenance to keep the facility in good working order and attractive to customers.

My goal isn't to give you an exhaustive list of alternative growth investments, but rather to teach you to think outside the box. Do your homework, and you'll see a world of opportunity beyond what you're taught by Suze Orman and *Money* magazine.

> **"Do more and more with less and less until eventually you can do everything with nothing."**
> —BUCKMINSTER FULLER

CHAPTER 19

A s your cash flow from your Growth investments grows, you'll be in a position to start considering Momentum investments. You're probably not in a position yet to even think about Momentum investing, and you may not be for a few years. Still, this section will help to paint a vision of what's possible and give you something to look forward to.

Until you've established a foundation of Growth investments, don't consider Momentum investments. This is a case where "When the student is ready, the teacher will appear." Once you've achieved financial independence with conservative Growth investments, you'll be astounded by how many opportunities arise with Momentum investments.

Remember, Momentum investments have a very high upside potential. But never invest funds you cannot afford to lose.

Whereas Growth investments have a higher probability of providing consistent cash flow, Momentum investments typically pay out in one lump sum (for example, investments in tech startups, angel investing, bio stocks, IPOs, etc.). When you do get a lump-sum payout, my recommendation is to reinvest and recycle those earnings back into a Growth investment to convert the cash into long-term cash flow.

The principle here is that, by funding Momentum investments with the revenue generated from Growth investments, we remove emotions from the equation. Your Growth investments have been funded by your hard work and are emotionally connected to you. You want to be conservative with that money. Momentum investments, however, are one step removed from your hard work and emotionally disconnected.

If you invest cash that was generated by a Growth investment and lose it all, you'll continue receiving cash flow from the Growth investment. If a Momentum investment pays out big, that's great. You now have more money to invest. But if it fails, then you haven't put yourself in any financial jeopardy. I recommend allocating a percentage of funds that you feel comfortable with in all Momentum investing.

Just because you're in a position to potentially lose everything you put into a Momentum investment doesn't mean you're gambling with this money. Gambling is based on a strong emotion of greed combined with a lack of understanding of what you are doing. In this case, you're being completely cool-headed, calculating, and strategic.

As with Growth investments, you're not following the crowd with Momentum investments and investing in what everyone else is investing in. You're still looking for alternative investments that give you greater control, more tax advantages, and higher potential for profit than you'll find from conventional sources.

My strong recommendation is that you don't start investing in Momentum vehicles until you've developed a 2:1 Passive Income Ratio, where you have a cash flow contingency and buffer. You'll have twice the amount of passive income than you need to cover your monthly expenses (plus, you may still have an active income as well). This puts you on safe ground to invest with confidence.

With that said, below are a few types of alternative Momentum investments to explore. Again, this is not an exhaustive list, nor is it detailed.

Business Startups

Business startups that are growing fast often need capital to fund inventory, purchase orders, and build vital infrastructure. Bootstrapping entrepreneurs have put in a lot of sweat equity in building their business to the point where it's ready for an investment. As an investor, you can acquire a percentage of the business without doing any of the physical work. The business owner gets capital to grow the business, and you participate in the profits when and if the business succeeds, based on your percentage of ownership. If you pick the right business and hit a home run, the investment could yield 5 to 100 times your initial investment.

As with any investment, performing proper due diligence to mitigate risk is crucial, including the following:

Invest in What You Know

If you're not passionate about food and know nothing about running a restaurant, that's probably not the best investment for you. By sticking with what you know, you have a much better understanding of the potential pitfalls the business may face and the blind spots the owner(s) may not be aware of. Furthermore, this gives you more control as an investor because you can add value to the process.

> "Know what you own, and know why you own it."
>
> —PETER LYNCH

Invest in People

The people behind the company are far more important than any other factor, including the business model and market potential. Know whom you're investing in. Study their experience and track records. Understand what value they bring to the table.

Understand the Financials

How does the business make money? Is it profitable? If not, is there a clear path to profitability? Are the projections realistic? Does the pricing make sense? Is it in line with market demand? If it is a listed company, what is the return on equity?

Don't just focus on the earnings per share. A deeper understanding of the operating business allows for a viable forecast of future business expectations. Are the profit margins significantly high? What is the real value of the stock? If the company stock is trading at less than its intrinsic value, the market may be indicating that the stock is undervalued, representing a buying opportunity.

Study the Market

Is the market big enough for the company to grow? Is the business truly solving a problem in the marketplace? Analyze the competition. Does the business have a competitive advantage? Is the company in tune with customer needs, and is it adapting to the market and fine-tuning its offers quickly?

Use these five steps to study the market:

1. Define a large demographic with a real problem you can solve.
2. Ask if this group of people would pay to have their problem solved.
3. Ask them to pay you to solve their problem.
4. Figure out the process in solving their problem.
5. Develop a scalable model for solving the problem.

Scalability

Is the business scalable? How can it grow large enough and quickly enough to pay back your investment with a return?

Research the Use of Funds

How does the company plan on using your investment? Is it really what it needs to grow to the next level? Does the founder's vision align with yours? How much does the owner intend on paying him or herself? Is it a reasonable salary for a startup, or is he or she being prematurely greedy?

Review the Legal Documents

Look at the articles of incorporation, bylaws, and any other relevant documents to understand how the company is structured and who is involved.

Private Equity Investments

Private equity investments are essentially investing in startups, but they are administered by firms that specialize in acquiring equity ownership in companies. Investing in a private equity fund usually requires a $250,000 minimum investment and can sometimes require up to $1 million or even more.

This can be a good way to go if you don't have the time or knowledge to personally invest in companies yourself. Private equity firms with experience, training, and skill perform all the due diligence on business opportunities. They use your investment to acquire business ownership and pay you a return based on the performance of the businesses within the fund.

Initial Public Offerings (IPOs)

An Initial Public Offering (IPO) is the process in which a privately owned company becomes a publicly traded company on the stock market with its initial sale of stock. The common shares are made available to outside investors on a public stock exchange. Essentially, companies that do this are securing capital to expand their business, purchase assets, or pay off debt.

For investors, the market for initial public offerings is mixed. Some IPOs are riskier than others and some have more potential for higher rewards. First-day returns for popular IPOs are usually high due to their speculative nature and high demand. Some IPOs have underperformed for years after going public.

One share of Google in 2004 at its initial public offering price was $85. Google is up 1,700 percent since its IPO. Opening shares of LinkedIn closed at $94.25, about 109 percent above the $45 IPO price. Facebook's IPO shares closed at $38.23. In its second full week of trading on June 1, the stock was valued at $27.72 per share. By June 6 original Facebook investors had lost a total of $40 billion. Facebook did not trade over $38 until fifteen months later. Groupon is still not profitable, and its share price is down considerably since its IPO in November 2011.

For investors wanting to get into IPO investing, it may be prudent to wait for the initial IPO hype to fade before acquiring the stock. This may mean buying the stock three months after it starts trading. After a few months the price of the stock moves more according to market fundamentals than the speculative hysteria preceding it.

Some investors assume an IPO is an opportunity to get in on the ground floor. In reality, prior to its IPO, a company may have secured multiple rounds of investments. By the time you acquire shares of a company during the IPO, early private institutional investors are existing shareholders.

Pre-IPO Funds

A pre-IPO fund's investment strategy is straightforward: Accredited investors purchase shares of a company before it is ready to issue an initial public offering. The investors plan to sell publicly after the IPO and capture any potential profit. You can get involved in pre-IPO funds by joining an angel investment group, or investing in a hedge or venture capital fund that invests in startup companies.

The investment in an unlisted company (pre-IPO) presents a risk of partial or total loss of capital. Do your due diligence and look for companies to invest in that have completed the riskiest phases of their product development. Ensure the company has achieved proof of concept on the technical and commercial level of product development. Invest only in companies where you understand the product sector and its business model. Never invest money that you might need over the short or medium term.

Purchasing Distressed Businesses

There are plenty of opportunities to buy businesses from struggling owners who don't know how to make their business profitable. If you have experience, knowledge, and skill in the domain of that business, you may be able to acquire it, raise the value, and turn it around within a relatively quick period, and either hand it off to managers or sell it at a profit. Just as homeowners who can't make payments are willing to sell their homes at steep discounts, distressed business owners do the same.

Creating value is a fundamental goal of all business acquisition. The value of the business creates intrinsic wealth when you increase its value and its multiples. Incorporating this methodology, the earnings before interest, taxes, depreciation, and amortization (EBITDA) from the business are multiplied by a multiple. For example: If a business has an EBITDA of $2 million and other similar businesses sell with an average multiple of three times earnings, that would suggest a business valuation of $6 million.

Real Life Story

Marshall Gibbs is a dentist who also loves investing in real estate and building businesses. Over the past several years, he has focused his efforts on purchasing distressed dental practices and turning them around. He started by purchasing an underperforming dental practice in 2014. When he bought it, it was doing about $900,000 per year in total revenues. Within one year, he built it up to $1.9 million. He started working part-time in the office, then brought in two other doctors, enabling him to stop working there.

Next, he found another underperforming practice that was doing about $350,000 per year. Within a year, he expanded it to about $800,000. In 2017, the opportunity to purchase a third practice came up. The real estate appraised for $900,000, but Marshall was able to negotiate a deal to buy it for $530,000. The dental practice had essentially been dissolved, so Marshall has been building it up from scratch. He collected $30,000 the first month of practice.

With each of these practices, Marshall has branded them with his "Mint Condition Dental" brand. He told us, "I've been inserting doctors as we go, with a long-term strategy of exiting and becoming more of a support organization where I can offer the doctors ownership, if they want it. So it's been rapid growth, but also positioning myself for those different outlets of passive income. Personally, I love real estate. I'll always hold onto the real estate because I have a long-term tenant now in each of those locations. So I get the rental income from the real estate, plus I'm able to collect trademark fees from the brand name."

Currently, he's only working as a dentist three days per week. He's negotiating a fourth deal with a dentist who needs to close her practice because of health issues and who's willing to seller finance the business. He says, "I see dentists come out of school with student debts of $500,000 or more, and they don't even know how to manage a business. That creates a lot of opportunity for me to work on the business instead of in it by helping dentists on the business side. That generates different avenues of cash flow for me."

Gold and Silver Speculation

As an avid investor in precious metals, I speculate on silver and, with the proceeds of any potential profits, I continue to add to my long-term gold reserves. Both metals can also be used as a hedge against inflation.

I determine my gold and silver purchases based on the gold-to-silver ratio, which is the amount of silver it takes to purchase one ounce of gold. The biblical (323 BC) gold-to-silver ratio was 12.5:1. During the height of the Roman Empire, the gold-to-silver ratio was 12:1. The historical 2,000-year-old average remains at 16:1. When the ratio is above 40:1, silver is the favored metal to buy. When the ratio is low and below 40:1, it's a signal to sell silver and buy gold bullion.

To formulate the gold-to-silver ratio, simply calculate the price of gold (per ounce) and divide it by the price of silver (per ounce). Here is an example: $1,343 (gold price) ÷ $21.60 (silver price) = approximately 62.18:1 (gold-to-silver ratio). In this example, silver is undervalued and primed for acquisition.

Cryptocurrencies

Cryptocurrency is a decentralized digital cash system that uses cryptography to secure transactions. Considered to be the money of the future, it has become a global phenomenon, not only in the tech industry but also in the investment sector.

Cryptocurrency is not issued by any central authority, which renders it immune to any government interference or manipulation. They regulate themselves and are governed by the laws of mathematics. Cryptocurrencies make it easier to transfer funds between two parties in a transaction, and with minimal processing fees compared to the steep fees charged by most financial institutions. The adoption rate of cryptocurrencies is increasing daily with banks, corporations, and governments recognizing its mainstream popularity.

The current leading cryptocurrencies are Bitcoin, Ethereum, Litecoin, Monero, Dash, and Ripple. A popular way to buy and sell cryptocurrencies and create your own digital currency "wallet" is to use a platform like Coinbase.com or Bittrex.com. Speculative investors should be aware there are risks involved in the investment and use of cryptocurrencies, such as fraud and security of the platforms. Cryptocurrencies can be electronically stolen, and there is no recourse for the individual. Other ways to invest in cryptocurrencies include either mining them or participating in an Initial Coin Offering (ICO) of new crypto coins.

Investing in cryptocurrencies, like all Momentum investments, means higher potential returns and higher potential losses. There's a lot of volatility, which creates trading opportunities. And there's been a big market run-up. Yet, cryptocurrencies will continue to have significant long-term potential.

 For more information on cryptocurrencies, visit 5DayWeekend.com. **Code: P12**

Wrap Up

In conclusion, I want to stress that you should reinvest all proceeds from Momentum investments back into cash flow–optimized Growth investments that pay a steady cash flow. If you strike gold with a Momentum investment or land a unicorn tech startup with a $1 billion valuation, you don't want to treat it like winning the lottery and spend all that cash on toys and vacations.

All liabilities should be purchased using your solid foundation of cash-flowing assets. These assets continually replenish your bank account. Don't spend down large lump sums of cash. Rather, continue reinvesting your investment proceeds to continue growing your asset base and cash flow.

> **"If you risk nothing then you risk everything."**
> —GEENA DAVIS

CHAPTER 20

WHY CONVENTIONAL INVESTMENTS FAIL

Conventional thinking and conventional investments simply can't deliver your 5 Day Weekend. They are designed as thirty-year retirement plans, and as such, their philosophy is at odds with the 5 Day Weekend. 5 Day Weekenders operate on completely different fundamental assumptions. Our objective is to find investments that give us passive cash flow now, rather than accumulating for future cash flow. We want control over our financial destiny.

Why Conventional Investments Can't Deliver

With 5 Day Weekend Investments, You . . .	With Conventional Investments, You . . .
• Create a financial foundation that provides liquidity	• Accumulate savings over your lifetime
• Build passive cash flow quickly	• Invest with stocks, mutual funds, 401(k)s, and IRAs
• Make investments that you control	• Rely on outside advisors, long-term stock market changes
• Develop an entrepreneurial lifestyle	• Work in a job as an employee for a company
• Become free in a few years	• Become free in 40-plus years

Here are some details about why conventional investments can't deliver your 5 Day Weekend:

No Immediate Cash Flow

Retail investments, which are standard investments you would buy from a broker, are based on a "set it and forget it" mentality. Sock money away into something you don't really understand, and let it sit for decades before you touch it. Hopefully, in that time it has grown beyond what you've contributed. Then you withdraw cash for retirement.

Financial institutions want your money. They want it on a regular, systematic basis and want to hold onto it for as long as possible with penalties imposed for early withdrawals. If an investment isn't intended to give you immediate cash flow, it's rigged in favor of financial institutions.

There are much better investments that give you immediate cash flow so you can accelerate your 5 Day Weekend lifestyle.

No Control

In a report on CBS's *60 Minutes* examining 401(k)s,[17] the question was asked, "What kind of retirement plan allows millions of people to lose 30 to 50 percent of their life savings just as they near retirement?"

Good question. The answer was 401(k)s. Unlike other investments that are protected from losses, your 401(k) rises and falls with the stock market, over which you have absolutely no control. Do you want to live your life worrying if the market will cooperate?

401(k)s are just one example of many conventional "investments" over which you have very little, if any, control. How much control do you have over the performance of mutual funds, for example? Any investment that doesn't enable you to personally add value and directly influence its return is something you should stay away from.

Bad Math

Financial advisors and pundits are notorious for using hypothetical scenarios to sell you products. Consider this example from author Richard Paul Evans: "Remember, if you are able to save just $100 a month and you faithfully transfer it to your nest egg, in forty years (compounded at the average S&P 500 rate of 10.2 percent) that little extra saving will be worth close to $700,000!"[18]

There's a glaring problem with this example and many others just like it. It glosses over the fact that, in order for it to work out this way, you have to get a steady, year in and year out 10.2 percent return. But that's not how the market works. The market goes up and down. An average return of 10.2 percent is far different than a steady 10.2 percent return.

Lack of Liquidity

Money in a 401(k) is tied up with penalties for early withdrawal unless you know how to safely navigate obscure IRS codes. This means you can't spend or invest your money to enrich your life without great difficulty and/or taking a big financial hit. The only exception allows you to borrow a limited amount of money from your 401(k) if you promise to pay it back. This automatically leads to double taxation and a slew of other negatives, the worst being if you lose your job or your income dries up, the deal changes and you must repay the loan within sixty days.

The theory behind 401(k)s is you keep putting money away, where you can't easily touch it without penalty, for thirty years, and it will compound into enough to retire on. We've seen why you should be suspicious of that story.

But here's the other problem: Money left to compound unpredictably for thirty years is stagnant money. There's no cash flow ready to direct to today's best uses. Instead, it's sitting still inside one thirty-year bet, while newer, better opportunities may be passing you by. What happens if you find a real estate deal that could make you $30,000 in thirty days, but you can't buy it because your cash is locked up in your 401(k)?

Tax Exposure

Retirement planners, reactive tax preparers, and pundits love touting the tax benefits of 401(k)s and IRAs. But most of these standard investments are tax-deferred, meaning you avoid paying taxes today by committing to paying them later. Taxes are historically low compared to the days of 50, 60, or even 90 percent marginal rates of the past. Chances are, with record national debt, taxes are eventually going up. If you don't like paying taxes today, why would you want to pay more taxes in the future?

It's ironic that people anticipate that they'll have healthy returns on their qualified plan while at the same time figuring they'll be in a lower tax bracket at retirement. If you have achieved any measure of success, you should actually be in a higher tax bracket at retirement. Most advisors, however, assume the opposite. Even worse, those higher tax brackets are likely to be even higher and more daunting in the future.

The tax deferral aspect of the 401(k), which is touted as a great boon, is actually a primary factor contributing to the underutilization of 401(k) funds. When the time finally comes to enjoy or live off the money, retirees are incentivized to let the money sit for fear of triggering burdensome tax consequences.

Other conventional investments, such as mutual funds, give you no tax benefits at all; you have to pay taxes on all your gains. The more sophisticated investments I use enable me to take advantage of IRS codes to defer taxes indefinitely or even get access to tax-free growth *and* tax-free withdrawals on the back end.

Diversify vs. Focus

Diversification is touted as a great risk-management strategy. Throw your money into a bunch of stuff. Some investments will lose money, others will gain. With luck, you'll come out ahead on the whole. The greatest risk of all, however, is ignorance—and diversification is by definition an admission of ignorance. People diversify because they don't know what will work, they have little or no control, and they can't or don't know how to add value to an investment. This isn't investing; it's gambling.

Diversification is another way of telling the "investor" that he doesn't have to think; he can just throw money in and good things will happen. This is clearly a philosophy for the ignorant. Ironically, the institutions that want us to believe this teach it as a way to reduce their own risk: The more risk we take, the less risk they have.

> The only way to properly invest is to focus.

Know what you're buying. Know how you can add value. Know how to control the outcome of the investment. Knowledge is power. And it also creates profit.

Furthermore, the sequential steps of the 5 Day Weekend plan make diversification obsolete. People get into diversification, like investing in mutual funds, when they skip foundational steps. In contrast, my advice is first, get your financial house in order. Get your protection in place, create liquidity, set up your wealth accounts, and start generating entrepreneurial income. Then, focus on specific Growth investments. Speculative Momentum investments don't come until much later.

Typical diversified investments are actually speculative in nature, meaning you don't have any certainty that they'll pay off for you. When you diversify as promoted by mainstream media, advisors, and pundits, you can actually create *more* risk instead of reducing it. You're doing things out of order. You're starting to speculate before having your foundation in place.

No Inflation Hedge

Inflation is the devaluation of currency as the Fed prints more and more money. It is usually reported to average about 3 percent per year, meaning every dollar you earn is worth less and less.

Conventional investments provide zero inflation hedge. Even if a mutual fund grows by 10 percent in one year, not only do you have to pay taxes on that growth, but also it's not really worth as much as you think because of inflation.

One example of an inflation hedge is rental properties. As inflation rises, you can raise your rent to compensate. And that's something you have direct control over. You don't have to cross your fingers and hope and pray the market performs well enough to compensate for inflation.

Another example is business ownership. As inflation rises, you can raise your prices on your products and/or services to offset inflation.

Inflation plays an integral part in determining the health of an economy. The government manipulates data and systematically underreports the true level of inflation. The government-issued consumer price index (CPI) has remained in low single digits for the last decade. But real economic data suggests otherwise. Devaluation of money, higher taxes, increased college tuition, rising housing prices, increased rents, higher costs of living, and exorbitant health insurance suggest the real inflation rate could be running as high as 7 percent annually.

Inflation, the invisible assassin, cannot be seen or felt. This stealthy predator loiters unabated by killing the purchasing power of your hard-earned after-tax dollars. No money actually leaves your bank account. Yet every single day, your purchasing power is being stolen from you. Inflation is dangerous. In fact, $1 in 1913 is worth about $.03 today. After moving from the gold standard to our current fiat currency system, a $100,000 savings in 1971 only has the purchasing power of $16,667 today. In light of inflation, there are other considerations that erode your purchasing power:

- Planned obsolescence: Products needing to be constantly replaced
- Technological advances: Future purchases that don't even exist today

As a rule of thumb you should ensure that you generate a minimum return of 7 percent per year growth to combat inflation. Anyone achieving less than 7 percent is going backwards. This is how the American middle class has been economically obliterated. (Be aware that most advisors don't account for inflation in their calculations.)

The Best Way to Invest

The investments I recommend are much different from anything you'll hear on financial shows on TV, which are designed to separate people from their money. If you trust the so-called experts, you'll forgo the 5 Day Weekend lifestyle in the name of sacrifice and deferral. Retail investments have horrific failure rates for investors.

> Most people are brainwashed by financial "gurus" who pitch either get-rich-quick schemes or get-rich-slow products.

I don't want you to hand off money to institutions and hope and pray they'll work out without knowing what you're doing. I don't want you to have to depend on the market cooperating to achieve lifestyle freedom. I want you to own your destiny. I want you to be free within five to ten years instead of thirty to forty.

To achieve this requires that you think like the wealthy do— outside the box of "buy, hold, and pray." The accumulation theory of investing (save money in tax-deferred vehicles and let it grow) will *not* create a 5 Day Weekend for you. Instead, consider cash-flowing investments as an alternative to what you've been taught. Focusing on cash flow is the path to true financial independence.

Think Outside the Box

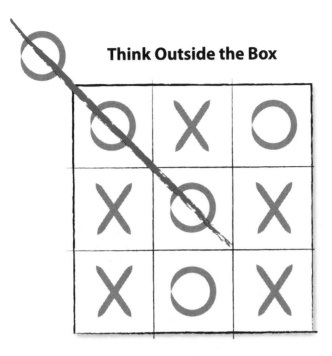

"The most dangerous phrase in the language is 'We've always done it this way.'"

—GRACE HOPPER

CHAPTER 21

SEASONS OF INVESTING

$\mathbf{F}$armers know there is a season for everything. They plant in the spring, cultivate in the summer, harvest in the fall, and fields lay dormant in the winter.

Economists are also familiar with seasons and cycles. There is a natural, measurable, and predictable ebb and flow to economic activity. Most cycles are driven by human emotions—primarily fear, greed, and indecision. When you understand these cycles, you can invest with much greater confidence and clarity. You can calm down your own emotions and do the opposite of what most emotion-driven investors are doing.

For the past twenty years I've been using a methodology for gauging the economy that has allowed me to accurately predict economic seasons. I compare economic cycles to the climatic seasons of summer, fall, winter, and spring, and overlay these cycles on an "economic clock" with times ranging from 1:00 to 12:00. I use this knowledge to determine the economic "temperature" and judge which investments are the best for each season.

Consider the diagram below:

Economic Clock

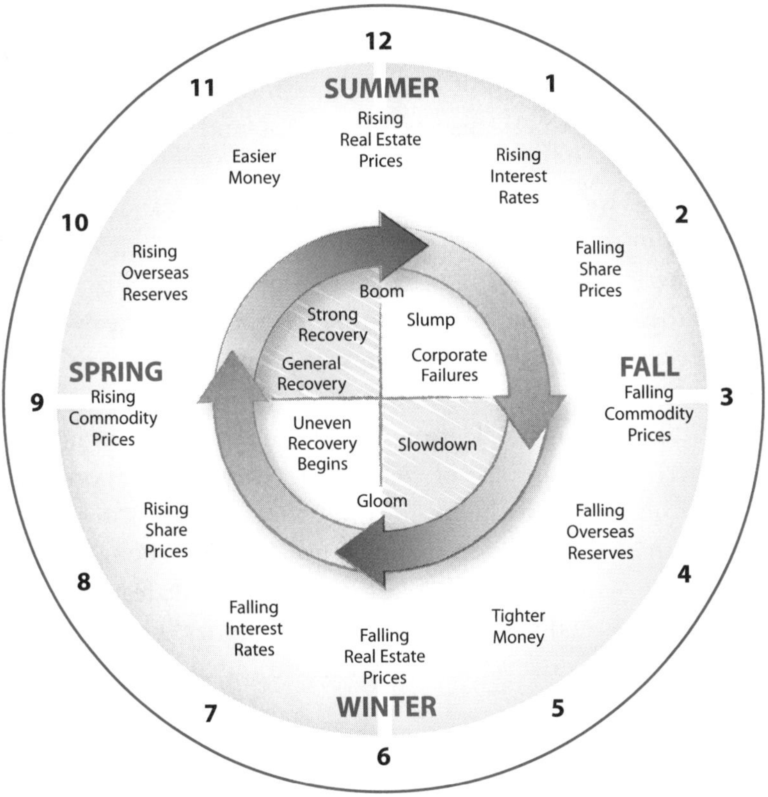

Let's start with 12:00, which is the height of the economic season of summer. The temperature is hot and simmering. It's economic boom time and the overall consumer sentiment is buoyant. The economy is flush with cash, just as the season of summer is flush with more daylight. Inflation is running hot, and it's officially the market peak and top of the economic boom.

At 3:00 we have the fall, marking the transition from summer into winter, with temperatures cooling considerably. Just as leaves fall in autumn, in economic terms we experience falling share prices, commodity prices, and overseas reserves. Money becomes scarce as monetary policy is tightened.

At 6:00 the economy is in winter, the coldest climatic season. There is a lack of confidence in the economy, and investors hibernate by waiting on the sidelines, eagerly awaiting an economic recovery. Winter is the depth of the recession. It is in this barren period that property foreclosures and business bankruptcies are at their peak. When the dust settled from the financial collapse of 2008, $5 trillion in pension money, real estate value, 401(k)s, savings, and bonds had disappeared. Eight million Americans lost their jobs and six million lost their homes.

At 9:00 we enter spring. We have rising prices and an overall recovery in the global economy. Spring is the breeding season of consumer confidence and the easing of monetary policy. Spring is also the market absorption of property stock from the oversupply of economic winter, when many developers failed to sell their properties.

A full economic cycle, from 12:00 back to 12:00 (summer to summer), covers a range of eight to eleven years. A boom/bust cycle, from 12:00 at the top of the boom (summer) to 6:00 at the depth of the recession (winter), usually takes about three to four years. When it comes to human emotion, the fear of losing money is greater than the greed of making money. That's why the markets reverse downwards like an elevator, creating widespread panic and selling.

Economic Indicators to Watch For

Consider the following chart, which outlines indicators that emerge at different times on the economic clock:

Here are the broad trends to watch for:

- **12:00–3:00** Real estate values are in decline. The economy is slowing down.
- **5:00** Property foreclosures and small business bankruptcies increase.

- **3:00–6:00** Unemployment, contraction of world economies, and recession.
- **4:00–6:00** Stocks enter a bear market. More profitable to develop property. Property landlords achieve higher rents.
- **6:00** Depth of the recession.
- **6:00–9:00** Recovery phase of the economy.
- **7:00** Banks and lenders free up liquidity. Period of bank expansion.
- **10:00** Increased building activity. Development and absorption of vacant land.
- **11:00** Easier credit and access to money.
- **9:00–12:00** Boom phase of the economy.

Time	Economic Status	Economic Result
1:00	Rising interest rates	Steady growth and inflation
2:00	Falling share prices	Falling profits and subdued confidence
3:00	Falling commodity prices	Construction in decline
4:00	Falling overseas reserves	Funds passed between central banks
5:00	Tighter money	Access to credit is scarce
6:00	Falling real estate prices	Property decline and recession
7:00	Falling interest rates	Economic stimulus
8:00	Rising share prices	Increased profits and confidence
9:00	Rising commodity prices	Construction increasing
10:00	Rising overseas reserves	Funds passed between central banks
11:00	Easier money	Borrowing becomes easier
12:00	Rising real estate prices	Top of the boom

What Drives Economic Cycles

I've been studying human behavior in relation to the economic emotions that create the economic cycles since I started investing as a teenager. What I've discovered is that specific emotions are the catalysts and drivers that alter the economic landscape of supply and demand, boom and bust. Three primal traits stand out above all else: greed, fear, and indecision.

Watch for Greed Between 8:00 and 1:00

Between 8:00 and 1:00 of the economic clock, the emotion in play is greed. With the easing of the monetary policy and with economic spring in motion, the banking sector is eager to lend funds. Borrowers follow the usual path of leveraged returns and can access up to 100 percent of the purchase. They start to accumulate debt until their debt levels hit record heights around 12:00.

Banks love to lend between 8:00 and 11:00; it's a no-brainer for them. The wholesale rate of cash versus the lending interest rate to borrowers ensures massive profits for banks. Unfortunately, speculative investors fuel the bonfire of insanity at 12:00. The economic party is winding down, and they predictably pay exorbitantly high prices for real estate. They soon find themselves upside down on their loans at 3:00. They owe more on their

Fear & Greed

properties than they are worth. Lots of foreclosures are about to hit the market.

Watch for Fear Between 1:00 and 6:00

Fear rules here, as the first sign of a slump appears and recession is on the horizon. Corporate failures are increasing and Wall Street is becoming nervous in this fall season. Share prices begin their decline. The selloff of shares and the subsequent downturn eventually flows onto the property market, a lagging indicator.

The speculative excess of summer and the insanity that ensues is prevalent. Banks significantly tighten up monetary supply at 5:00. The cash flow that lubricates the economy has stalled, and we hit the depth of the recession at 6:00—characterized by high unemployment, bankruptcies, and panic.

Indecision Governs Between 6:00 and 8:00

Here, the economic recovery is slow to start. As an investor, I eagerly await 7:00. This is when banks and lenders start to free up liquidity. They need to increase profits. Most people are still licking their financial wounds and are hesitant and indecisive. Quantitative easing is in full force and central banks are attempting to resuscitate the economy with the printing press. Wall Street commences a bullish run, in anticipation of more buoyant economic conditions, and acts as a leading indicator.

The media will provide the bright spark consumers are longing to hear. The banking sector lowers interest rates to incentivize investors to come in from the cold. At 8:00, we have easier credit and access to money. The road to economic spring is just around the corner.

How to Invest in Each Season

By understanding the thermostat of economic seasons, we can anticipate what will happen next and take advantage of it with our investing. Here's what to do in each season:

> "The four most dangerous words in investing are: 'this time it's different.'"
>
> —SIR JOHN TEMPLETON

Economic Summer

In summer you need to become cash-flow rich for the next expected cycle of fall. The economy is lubricated with cash, and credit borrowing and companies tend to become fat and overweight. Spending is at an all-time high and most of it is indiscriminate. Just like the actions of a seasonal farmer, you must have hay in the shed to last you through the winter. Economic behavior is no different.

As a Business Owner

In economic summer, trim the fat from your business for the expected fall. Tighten expenditures and reign in the credit cards. Ensure you have ample cash-flow reserves to act as a buffer for the business. Don't wait for the winter, during the depth of the recession, to resuscitate your business. It will be too late.

As a Property Investor

You should not be acquiring properties in economic summer. If you plan to sell, now is the opportune time; it's a seller's market. The economic party is nearing its inevitable end. There is widespread speculation and insanity in the property marketplace. Auction clearance rates of properties are at record levels, and there is an overwhelming sense that things are getting out of control. Demand is far outstripping supply. Banks are nervous and, in order to take the heat out of the market, they increase interest rates. With a speculative environment, 100 percent mortgages or no-money-down property deals are all the buzz and rage.

When you start attending weddings and parties and everyone is talking about investing—RUN. You know the party has ended and we have just arrived at 1:00 in the economy. When the taxi driver at the airport picks you up and offers investment advice, then you know it's 2:00. Beware of friends who are high on advice but low on financial results at this point. Some criticize others to conceal their own fear and justify their lack of accomplishment.

Economic Winter

The economy is barren and many world economies are hemorrhaging. Banks have very little confidence in consumers' ability to service the debt they absorbed in the speculative season of summer. Consumer spending is at an all-time low and high unemployment prevails. The great transfer of wealth from the financially uneducated to the educated is highly evident. There is an epidemic of market oversupply. Savvy individuals exploit this economic opportunity. Bargain hunters make a killing.

As a Business Owner

You plan for the summer in winter. You buy out your competitors between the fall (3:00) and winter (6:00). It's not their products you seek, but access and ownership of their customers and databases. Companies you buy out in this economic season did not save enough cash flow in the summer, and therefore they could not ride out the economic winter.

The health of your business is determined in winter. Your customers think differently in winter as their purchases are based upon their low cash reserves. They are reluctant to spend. Change what you sell and offer your best deals in winter.

As a Property Investor

You should be acquiring as many properties as you can in winter. The cash flow surplus you saved in summer will allow you to purchase properties at fantastic deals.

Auction clearance rates of properties are at very low levels, and there is an overwhelming sense of economic hardship. There is much more supply than demand of property stock. It's the depth of the recession, the market bottom, and a buyer's market. Property developers are desperate to off-load apartments and houses. Property foreclosures are at record highs once again, with owners not able to meet mortgage obligations or pay their property taxes.

Only those that are cashed up will reap this epic harvest of offerings at pennies on the dollar. Where there is crisis, there is always opportunity.

Here are specific actions to take at certain times on the economic clock:

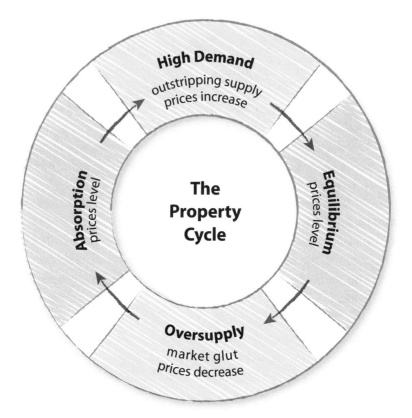

- **6:30** Increase stock share ownership.
- **9:00** Increase property ownership and reduce bonds.
- **12:00** Reduce stock share ownership, increase and secure cash reserves.
- **3:30** Increase property ownership and increase bonds.
- **3:00–6:00** Acquire and valufacture businesses. Increase profits with a predetermined exit window at 11:00 in economic summer. Sell businesses during the speculative window of summer. At 11:00, the economy is flush with cash, and buyers tend to overpay when acquiring businesses. Exit to generate quick profits, and plan to use this money at 3:00 when businesses start to fail due to poor management.
- **9:00–11:00** With bank loans, fix your interest rate for a minimum of five years. Between 12:00 and 1:00, interest rates generally increase. Refinance and fix your interest rate prior to that, then profit with lower repayments.

Market Cycles

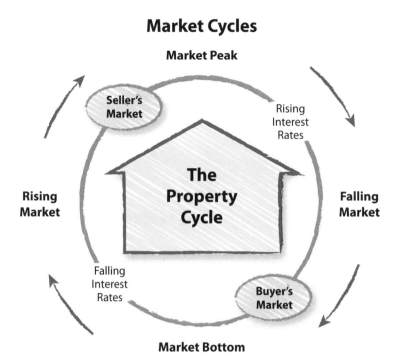

Market Peak

Seller's Market

Rising Interest Rates

Rising Market

The Property Cycle

Falling Market

Falling Interest Rates

Buyer's Market

Market Bottom

- **11:00** Have your properties revalued and access a line of credit with the bank. The property market at 11:00 is speculative and running hot. Property valuations are approaching record highs. Use the high valuation of your property portfolio in economic summer to your advantage. Exploit the weakness between the fall and winter seasons of bargain-priced properties that come onto the market. Have preapproved access to the banks' money at favorable interest rates.

> "Look at market fluctuations as your friend rather than your enemy; profit from folly rather than participate in it."
> —WARREN BUFFETT

Call to Action

Your Investing Plan

What season are we in now?

What time is it on the clock?

Which of the three Growth investment ideas intrigue you most?

What's your plan for researching and implementing these ideas?

Who in your life can be a resource in helping you learn and implement these ideas? Write down as many names as you can think of.

What's your plan for building relationships with these people? Be as specific as possible.

What's your next step?

Go to our website to download and print this worksheet at 5DayWeekend.com.
Code: P13

> "Rich people see every dollar as a 'seed' that can be planted to earn a hundred more dollars, which can then be replanted to earn a thousand more dollars."
>
> —T. HARV EKER

The reality is this: You won't achieve a 5 Day Weekend lifestyle as the same person you are today. The process is an internal journey as much, if not more, as an external journey.

There are things about yourself that you're going to have to address. Blind spots will be revealed. Weaknesses will be revealed and improved upon. Untapped strengths will be discovered and developed. It's going to take everything you've currently got—and more.

Becoming a 5 Day Weekend person can bring out the best in you. The practices in the following four chapters are critical to realizing your full potential.

CHAPTERS

- **Strengthen Your Mindset**

- **Build Your Inner Circle**

- **Fortify Your Habits**

- **Amplify Your Energy**

- *Call to Action*
  Your Power Up! Plan

CHAPTER 22

Your business idea could fail. You could lose money. People could make fun of you.

You may not have control over everything, but you have control over the one thing that matters most: your mindset. Success is an inside-out job. Your mindset is what keeps you going when everything seems hopeless. Your mindset can get you unstuck and keep you moving forward. Your mindset is what conquers challenges.

The right mindset is the foundation of all success.

Vital Components of a Strong Mindset

Commitment and Perseverance

Most people think that what's keeping them stuck is a lack of knowledge and skill. The reality is that any lack of knowledge, skill, or experience is easily compensated for through commitment and perseverance.

Millions of entrepreneurs have proven this countless times. Henry Ford had no idea how to build an auto empire—but that's exactly what he did. Chris Gardner knew nothing about being a stockbroker, but he hustled so hard that a movie was made about him (*The Pursuit of Happyness*). Oprah Winfrey had no experience in media until she got a job as a newsreader at a local radio station.

> "Success doesn't come from what you do occasionally; it comes from what you do consistently."
>
> —MARIE FORLEO

Successful people earn their way to the top—not through knowledge and skill, but through commitment and perseverance.

Believe in Yourself

Doubt says, "I'll believe it when I see it." Faith says, "I'll see it when I believe it." The most successful people have always had an abiding belief in themselves. No matter what challenges they faced, no matter what failures knocked them down, they just *knew* that they would succeed, no matter what.

Self-doubt kills more dreams than failure ever could. Before you can succeed, you have to believe that you're worthy of success and that you have what it takes. Believe it first, and it will manifest. When you alter your belief system, you change your biochemistry and physiology. Allow life to question you. Listen to your inner voice. There you can find the strength to believe in yourself.

Strengthening Your Mindset

1. Empower Your Mind

People become mentally weak because they don't counteract the pervasive negative voices of family, friends, and society. The only way to do this is to constantly fill your mind with positive, uplifting, inspiring, and educational content. Think of your mindset as a muscle—it must be exercised consistently. When you read, use a $100 bill as a bookmark to reinforce that there is a wealth of knowledge and money in every book you read.

> "Never undersell yourself unless you want everyone else to."
> —ELAINE DUNDY

2. Do What Scares You

The only way to conquer fear is to face it. Do what you fear enough times, and eventually you develop a confidence you never thought you had. Don't let your fear of what could happen make nothing happen.

> "Feel the fear and do it anyway."
> —SUSAN JEFFERS

3. Make Stress Your Friend

Stress is not your enemy; rather, it's a valuable tool and ally if you can harness its force. Your mental faculties are heightened when you are pushed against a tough problem or deadline. Stress is your body preparing to meet challenges. Don't fight stress— embrace it. See how it's helping you. Feed on its energy.

It should be noted that there's a difference between chronic versus temporary stress. If you're experiencing chronic stress, it's a sign you probably want to make major changes in your life. Constantly staying in stress mode causes adrenal fatigue. Temporary stress, however, can be our friend—if we allow our bodies to heal.

Your Limits — and Your Freedom — Are in Your Mind

It's been said so often that it's become cliché, but it's really true. Whether you think you can or you think you can't, you're right. Your limits are a product of your mindset. They can be stretched and freedom can be found by cultivating the right mindset.

> "You have power over your mind — not outside events. Realize this, and you will find strength."
> —MARCUS AURELIUS

CHAPTER 23

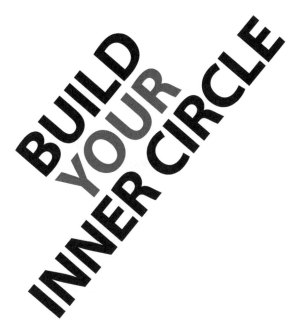

Few things have more impact on your level of success than your close inner circle—the people with whom you spend the most time, those from whom you seek guidance and counsel.

Vital Components of a Healthy Inner Circle

1. The Right Friends Push You Beyond Your Limits

The wrong friends allow you to be complacent. They ask nothing of you, other than that you don't push them out of their comfort zone. They want to "accept you as you are," but this is not true friendship at all. To them, your mediocrity justifies their own.

The right friends, in contrast, see you not only for who you are right now, but also for who you can become. They constantly push and inspire you to become better.

2. The Right Friends Hold You Accountable

The wrong friends accept your excuses and rationalizations, and even feed them. This is a counterfeit version of "support" — more accurately described as indulgence.

> "Don't make friends who are comfortable to be with. Make friends who will force you to lever yourself up."
>
> —THOMAS J. WATSON

True friends give you tough love. They never let you give up on your goals and dreams. They hold you to your word. They demand that you live up to your best. This is the kind of true support we should all seek from our closest friends.

3. The Right Friends Are Strivers and Achievers

It's easy to pick out the wrong friends. They haven't changed, improved, or achieved much within the last ten years.

The friends you want are those who are constantly striving to become better and achieve higher goals. Look at their lives over the past ten years. How far have they come? How many projects have they started? How many times have they failed? If they haven't failed much, it's because they're not doing much.

Keys to Building Your Inner Circle

1. Immediately Cut Ties with Toxic People

Toxic people are constantly negative and skeptical. They gossip and meddle in other people's business. They spend their time on cheap entertainment. Toxic people are dying of negativity. They just have to wait until they are eighty years old to make it official.

Your life is far too valuable to be dragged down by such people. If you have any friends like this, stop spending time with them. You have far better things to do with your time. Password-protect your brain and don't allow others to pollute it. One of the biggest costs to wealth is toxic people. One toxic person can counteract the advantages of ten amazing relationships.

2. Build Strong, Deep Relationships with a Vital Few

Find people who have the qualities of good friends mentioned previously, and do everything you can to get close to them.

It's often said that your net worth and income will never be greater than the average of those of the five people with whom you spend the most time. I really believe this is true. Befriend people who are more successful than you and who stretch you, rather than those who allow you to stay comfortable where you are. Find the dreamers and the doers. Associate with them as much as possible and learn from them.

3. Create a Formal Mastermind Group

In his fantastic book *Think and Grow Rich*, Napoleon Hill teaches "The Mastermind Principle," which he defines as "an alliance of two or more minds working in perfect harmony for the attainment of a common definite objective." A formal mastermind group meets on a regular basis to help one another overcome challenges and achieve goals.

4. Get a Formal Mentor

One of the fastest and simplest ways to achieve a financial goal is to learn from those who have already gone where you'd like to go. Mentors understand the path you want to tread. They know the pitfalls and dangers. They see your blind spots and weaknesses, as well as your strengths. You are the result of every decision you have made in your life. Without a mentor, your very best thinking has got you exactly where you are today.

No aspiring 5 Day Weekender should be without at least one formal mentor. Search diligently for the right one for you, then don't hesitate to reach out to him. Find ways to create value for him. Meet regularly to ask advice on your challenges and to get new insights. Never waste a mentor's time—heed his advice religiously.

5. Be the Friend You Want to Have

Ultimately, the best way to find the right friends is to *be* the right friend. We attract not what we want, but rather what we are.

Be all the things you look for in a friend who can take you to the next level. Never rest on your laurels. Always have goals written down and never stop striving to achieve them. Conquer your fears. Be positive and supportive. Never tear people down; always seek to build others up. By doing this, you will find it easy to build your trusted inner circle with the right people.

Create Your "Life Board"

You've probably heard of a "vision board," a board visually displaying your major life goals. Few people, however, have consciously created a "life board"—your personal board of directors who help you steer your life, conquer your obstacles, and achieve your goals. In many ways, this is more important than a vision board.

When you spend your time with the right people, your life is automatically elevated. Here's a social influence ratio that I suggest on how to spend your time:

- Spend 20 percent of your time mentoring others. This facilitates the reinforcement of knowledge and the understanding of it. Educating others feeds my heart. That is what is most emotionally profitable for me.
- Spend 30 percent of your time with people on the same wave frequency as you.
- Spend 50 percent of your time with people who are more experienced, knowledgeable, and successful than you. They

are years ahead of you, possibly even decades. They can inspire you to grow, adapt, and scale up your business and ideas. They can provide you with the formula for developing a business that supports your lifestyle, as opposed to a lifestyle that supports your business.

- If you want to continue pushing yourself to the next level, you must surround yourself with people who have a deep domain expertise and are playing at a higher level than you. Be in the orbit of individuals transmitting the highest frequency of wisdom. This is in contrast to those who blindly operate on 50/50/0 social influence ratio, devoid of any illuminating inspiration, experience, or wisdom.

Building your inner circle is less about expanding your relationships and more about tightening and deepening them. Quality matters in this case far more than quantity.

Creating a tight and valuable inner circle won't guarantee your success, but I can guarantee you won't succeed without it.

> **"Show me your friends, and I'll show you your future."**
> —DANNY HOLLAND

CHAPTER 24

Habits are a double-edged sword. On the one hand, they can be an incredibly powerful tool for progress. On the other hand, by automating our behavior, they erode our free will and make us less conscious. It's vital, therefore, that we remain vigilant about the habits we develop.

Charles Duhigg's book, *The Power of Habit*, details the science behind how habits form and how to change them. Close to the center of our skull, Duhigg explains, lies a golf ball–sized lump of tissue called the basal ganglia. Its job is to store habits even while the rest of our brain goes to sleep. Science has proven that repeated habits become ingrained into our basal ganglia forever. Our brain is programmed to constantly find new ways to save effort. As Duhigg writes, "Left to its own devices, the brain will try to make almost any routine into a habit, because habits allow our minds to ramp down more often."

Habits are born from a three-step loop: First, there is a cue, which is a mental trigger that flips your brain into automatic mode. Second, we fall into a routine. And third, by engaging in the routine, we give our brain a reward. When this loop is repeated over time (cue, routine, reward), it becomes increasingly automatic and becomes a habit.

Once born, habits never die. As MIT scientist Ann Graybiel says, "Habits never really disappear. They're encoded into the structures of our brain, and that's a huge advantage for us, because it would be awful if we had to relearn how to drive after every vacation. The problem is that your brain can't tell the difference between bad and good habits, and so if you have a bad one, it's always lurking there, waiting for the right cues and rewards."[19]

> "Sow a thought, reap an action; sow an action, reap a habit; sow a habit, reap a character; sow a character, reap a destiny."
> —STEPHEN R. COVEY

It's impossible to create the 5 Day Weekend lifestyle without having the right habits, or if you're governed by the wrong habits.

Vital Components of Strong and Healthy Habits

1. Healthy Habits Are Created Consciously

Unconscious habits tend to be formed by taking the path of least resistance, which is almost never good for us (e.g., sleeping in, eating junk food, watching too much TV, overspending, etc.).

The right habits are those that we consciously create and cultivate, such as healthy eating, daily exercise, and goal setting and planning. Conscious habits take more effort, but in the long run provide quantum benefits for the effort.

2. Healthy Habits Take Us Toward Our Goals

Positive daily habits such as reading inspirational and personal success books, listening to informative podcasts, and viewing instructional videos help us become more optimistic and knowledgeable. Exercising, meditating, doing volunteer work, and supporting friends add to the richness of our lives and support our goals.

Negative daily habits, such as constantly being connected to your smartphone and computer, wasting time on Facebook and other social media, negative self-talk, and using your credit card to feel better, hinder your progress toward your goals.

Do more positive. Do less negative.

3. Healthy Habits Support Overall Health and Well-Being

The right habits not only support you in achieving specific goals, but they also support your health and well-being in a general sense. In short, they are simply good for you. They make you smarter, healthier, more productive, and happier.

Any habit that diminishes your overall mental, emotional, and physical health should be eliminated.

Keys to Fortifying Good Habits

1. Develop a Morning Routine

One of the most important things you can ever do to change your life is to create a conscious morning routine. Use it to stoke your inner fire.

Make it a habit to get up an hour earlier than usual. Start your day with some breathing exercises and meditation. Take a walk in the morning sun. Read a nonfiction book or listen to podcasts. Visualize your goals. Work on a personal project you're passionate about. It doesn't matter what you do, so long as it's conscious, positive, and consistent. Don't allow the digital world to control your first hour of the day. Don't just prioritize your schedule for the day, schedule your priorities.

2. Lean on a Support Group

The research is clear: Our odds of changing a habit increase dramatically when we commit to changing as part of a group. The reason for this is that we must believe that change is possible. In a group, our belief in our ability to change is reinforced.

Your support group should know the habits you're working on breaking and those you're working on creating. Keep the group in the loop on your progress (or lack thereof). The simple act of accountability is often enough to motivate you to do better.

3. Focus on "Keystone" Habits

"Keystone" habits are seemingly small, simple habits, but which can initiate a ripple effect and have a major impact on every aspect of your life. One such keystone habit is exercise. As research shows, people who start exercising also start eating better, they're more productive at work, they smoke less, they

> "You will never change your life until you change something you do daily. The secret of your success is found in your daily routine."
> —JOHN MAXWELL

show more patience with colleagues and family, they use their credit cards less frequently, and they say they feel less stressed.

Other keystone habits could include completely cutting out TV, getting enough sleep, eliminating negative self-talk, and saving money. Or take one meditative road trip each month for a few days. Travel a minimum of 200 miles from your home to trigger a spark of business creativity.

Harness the Power of Habit

Habits can either work for or against you. They can propel you toward your goals, or prevent you from ever achieving them. If you allow your habits to form unconsciously, they will most likely work against you.

Consciously choose the habits you want to create. Work on them diligently and consistently. More than daily choices, habits are the building blocks of life.

"Motivation is what gets you started.
Habit is what keeps you going."
—JIM ROHN

CHAPTER 25

AMPLIFY YOUR ENERGY

In the '80s and '90s, time management was all the rave. Planners, Blackberries, and other time management tools abounded. New research has made time management almost obsolete. The new paradigm is that energy management matters far more.

This revolutionary approach to performance is detailed in the life-changing book *The Power of Full Engagement* by Jim Loehr and Tony Schwartz. They explain, "The richest, happiest and most productive lives are characterized by the ability to fully engage in the challenge at hand, but also to disengage periodically and seek renewal. Instead many of us live our lives as if we are running in an endless marathon, pushing ourselves far beyond healthy levels of exertion.... We...must learn to live our lives as a series of sprints."

In other words, achieving the 5 Day Weekend isn't just about working hard — it's about working smart. We don't manage time, we create it.

Vital Components of Effective Energy Management

1. Work with the Natural Rhythms of Your Body

Psychophysiologist Peretz Lavie was one of the early pioneers of the new research on energy management. His experiments showed that our energy functions according to "ultradian rhythms," or natural cycles that take place during the day. In the morning, we have a dip in energy every ninety minutes. In the afternoon and evening, we have an energy dip at 4:30 p.m. and at 11:30 p.m. These ninety-minute cycles are our ultradian rhythms, the times when we're feeling more alert and productive.

Research shows that by tapping into and working with our natural ultradian rhythms, we perform better. Instead of planning out our day and adhering to our schedule religiously, a more effective approach is to perform focused work in short bursts throughout the day.

2. Give Yourself Permission to Have Your Own Rhythms

Although research shows general patterns for ultradian rhythms, researchers also acknowledge that body clocks can vary widely. Contrary to the time management paradigm, it works best to adjust your schedule to fit your personal rhythms.

> Your greatest source of energy is being excited about your life and having a compelling vision for your future.

Our bodies are naturally hardwired to operate at our optimized rhythm. Tune into your own body's rhythms and allow yourself the flexibility to arrange your life accordingly. For example, your peak creative time may be between 7:00 and 9:00 a.m. If so, turn off your smartphone and all notifications, don't check email and social media then, and focus on your most important work.

3. Manage All Four Energy Quadrants

There are four sources of energy, or "quadrants": body, emotions, mind, and spirit. Each source is depleted and replenished in its own way, so you must pay attention to each one. You may be good at managing your body's energy, but if you neglect your spiritual energy, you still won't be functioning at optimal levels.

Keys to Amplifying Your Energy

1. Break Your Work into 90-Minute Blocks

Forget the standard 9-to-5 mentality. Learn your body's natural rhythms, and then schedule your most important and productive work in ninety-minute blocks. We need to renew our energy rhythm at ninety-minute intervals, not just physically, but also mentally.

Eliminate distractions and focus intently during these blocks. Then, take twenty-five-minute breaks at the end of each focused work block. Take a walk, walk the dog, get a snack, or just lie down. You might consider having a walking business meeting during a break for fresh air. Knowing you have a break coming up prevents burnout.

2. Create Recharging Rituals

Create recharging rituals for each of your four sources of energy (body, emotions, mind, spirit). For example:

- Body Rituals: regular walks, eating at certain times throughout the day, going to bed at a set time, playing sports
- Emotional Rituals: humor and laughter, expressing appreciation to others, spending time with friends
- Mental Rituals: shutting off your phone at certain times, reading, watching TED talks, practicing a new skill
- Spiritual Rituals: meditation, prayer, scripture reading

3. Optimize Your Sleep

Sleep isn't a necessary evil—a distraction from work. It's a vital component of our body's productivity, a natural way of recharging.

Listen to your body to determine the appropriate amount of sleep for you. The standard "eight hours per night" is more of a guideline; you may require more or less. I personally sleep six hours per day with a power siesta nap of twenty-five minutes seven hours after I wake up in the morning. This biphasic sleep pattern (six hours plus twenty-five minutes) is my ideal sweet spot. When you start feeling that afternoon crash, don't fight it with coffee or energy drinks—pay attention to your body and take a power nap. Taking a nap too late in the day can affect sleep quality. The short siesta nap increases alertness and improves memory and productivity during the evening hours.

> "Sleep is the best meditation."
> —DALAI LAMA

Go to bed at a designated time. One hour beforehand, turn off all electronic devices and avoid all stimulants and alcohol to help your body and mind wind down. Don't overstimulate your brain with screen time (TV, tablet, phone) right before bed. You will disorientate your circadian rhythm. As a result, it will take you longer to fall asleep, eroding the integrity of your rest time and disrupting the ability to awaken fully charged. Before going to sleep, take five minutes to list everything you need to do the next day.

4. Exercise Daily

Studies show that exercising boosts your energy. The more you move, the more energy you will feel. One study reports that inactive people who normally complain of fatigue could increase their energy by 20 percent and decrease fatigue by as much as 65 percent by engaging in regular, low-intensity exercise.[20] Other studies have shown energy is boosted more through exercise than by using stimulant medications.

5. Eat Healthy and Drink Enough Alkalized Water

Food is the fuel of your body. The higher quality fuel you put in your tank, the better you'll perform. Cut out sugar, sugary drinks (soft drinks, iced tea, etc.), and processed foods. Eat more vegetables and fruits.

Alkaline water neutralizes the acid in your body and increases oxygen levels. The guideline for drinking water with a minimum alkalized pH level of 8.0 is to drink between one-half to one ounce of water for each pound you weigh, every day. Considering the human body is around 60 percent water, I drink a minimum of ninety ounces per day. Upon waking, I drink a twenty-ounce bottle of chilled alkalized water to invigorate my mind and body.

Focus on the Most Important Things

Most people work a minimum of eight hours a day, although that often stretches to ten or twelve hours per day, especially when you consider commuting. The truth is that we don't have to work that long to accomplish great things. As I've said before, those who get paid to work, work for those who get paid to think.

> Busy people doing busy work do not make money. Productive people doing productive work make money.

The 5 Day Weekend lifestyle is about compressing and maximizing your productive time. With any given task, the work naturally expands to fill the time available for its completion. When you allocate an abundance of time to a task, it will consume that time. Allocate less time and you'll be far more productive.

> **"Energy and persistence conquer all things."**
> —BENJAMIN FRANKLIN

Call to Action
Your Power Up! Plan

Strengthen Your Mindset

Make a list of the next five books/audiobooks you plan to read or listen to. Which podcasts or video channels can you use?

Vision Board

Create a "vision board" using visual imagery. Post it in a place where you'll see it daily.

Build Your Inner Circle

Write down the names of the top five toxic people in your life who drag you down and create negativity and stress in your life. What is your plan for limiting your interactions with these people?

Write down the names of the top five people in your life who lift you up and bring out the best in you. What is your plan to deepen your relationships?

Write down the names of five people who share common goals with you. People you want to be in a formal mastermind group with you. What's your plan for creating your mastermind group?

Write down the names of three people whom you would love to have as mentors. What's your plan for building those relationships?

Fortify Your Habits

Create your ideal morning routine, whatever you would like to include (reading, prayer, meditation, visualization, exercise, etc.) to last for thirty minutes to an hour.

Amplify Your Energy

What are the hours during the day when you are at peak performance?

What are the most important things you should be doing during those hours?

What is your plan for optimizing these hours? Your recharging rituals?

What's your plan for being more conscious about using these rituals throughout your day?

What is your optimal sleep schedule?

What's your plan for sticking to this schedule?

What needs to change about your exercise regimen?

What needs to change about your diet?

Go to our website to download and print this worksheet at 5DayWeekend.com.
Code: P14

> "Life either happens by design or default. You choose."
> —BOB PROCTOR

The 5 Day Weekend is about reframing and re-envisioning the American Dream.

For far too long the American Dream has been defined in materialistic terms. You've "made it" when you have that nice, big, custom house; that fancy, shiny car; a swimming pool; four-wheelers; and other toys. But rarely does a high-consumption lifestyle come with real freedom. Many people are in debt up to their eyeballs and are slaves to their toys, with their accompanying loan payments. People who think they own a lot of liabilities find that their liabilities actually own *them*.

Enjoying a high standard of living is not the same thing as the lifestyle freedom I refer to in the 5 Day Weekend. I'm talking about the freedom to do what you want when you want, to pursue adventure and create unforgettable memories, to enjoy each moment without worrying about how you're going to pay your bills and feed your family, to live a life of purpose and significance. You are able to take an extended time away from your daily life to travel the world on your own terms.

My advice is to break free from society's demands and live the life of your choosing, rather than simply following the crowd and keeping up with the Joneses. The Joneses have never had it as good as you'll have it when you achieve your freedom.

CHAPTERS

- **Freedom from Stuck**

- **Freedom from Yes**

- **Freedom from Perfection**

- **Freedom from Stuff**

- **Freedom from Boredom**

- **Freedom from Regret**

- **Freedom from Self**

- *Call to Action*

  Your Freedom Lifestyle Plan

CHAPTER 26

A t the age of thirty-two, Bucky was in a deep depression after losing his job. He was wandering through life with no clear direction. He had been expelled from college twice and had drifted from one meaningless job to the next. With no income to support his family, debt was piling up.

Bucky started drinking heavily and wandered aimlessly through the streets of Chicago. On one such walk he arrived at the shore of Lake Michigan. He stared out at the water and seriously considered swimming out until he was too exhausted to swim anymore. With his life insurance policy, he thought, he was worth more dead than alive.

As he stood there, something happened that changed his life forever. He says he heard a voice declaring, "You do not have the right to eliminate yourself. You do not belong to you. You belong to the Universe. Your significance will remain forever obscure to you, but you may assume that you are fulfilling your role if you apply yourself to converting your experiences to the highest advantage of others."[21]

After this experience, Bucky chose to embark on "an experiment, to find what a single individual [could] contribute to changing the world and benefiting all humanity."[22] He became an architect, systems theorist, designer, inventor, and the author of more than thirty books, and he was hailed as "one of the greatest minds of our times."

A Clear Purpose Unleashes Your Greatness

As we learn from Buckminster Fuller, what keeps us stuck in life is a lack of purpose. Having a clear purpose unleashes the best in us and enables us to escape aimlessness, boredom, and mediocrity.

> "Don't ask yourself what the world needs. Ask yourself what makes you come alive, and go do that, because what the world needs is people who have come alive."
>
> —GIL BAILIE

5 Day Weekenders are men and women of purpose. They know who they are and what they stand for. They know what they're trying to do and how they will measure success. They stay focused on their purpose; they may change their plans, but their goals remain clear and fixed. Having five more days doesn't mean watching more TV. It means contributing more and having a greater impact.

Never lose the insatiable hunger in life. Those who remain hungry will dominate life at every turn. If you don't prioritize your life, someone else will.

Ways to Live on Purpose

1. Don't Find Your Purpose — *Create* It

From its roots, the word "purpose" literally means "to put forth an intention." Stop trying to find purpose, as if there's only *one* right path for you, one destiny lined out for you. What do *you* intend to do with your gifts? Create an intention and pursue it obsessively.

2. Find Your Gifts and Follow Your Bliss

Your purpose is what you want to do because it gives you the highest levels of joy and fulfillment. Stop asking, "How can I find my purpose?" and instead ask, "What purpose do I want to choose and create that will make me truly, deeply blissful?"

Forget about finding purpose—go find what makes you tick, what comes naturally to you. What are you good at? What do you enjoy doing? What makes you lose all track of time?

3. Life as a Professional, Not an Amateur

Amateurs make excuses about why they're not living up to their full potential. Professionals ditch the excuses and fully develop their talents and gifts. A natural aptitude may give you potential, but you must do the work to develop it. Sometimes following your bliss really means following your blisters—putting in the hard work, day after day, to become who you were born to become.

4. Do What You Fear

One of the greatest clues to purpose is what you fear the most. I'm not talking about primal fears like heights or snakes, but the fear of putting yourself out there and doing something you've never done before. Everything you want in life is on the other side of your fears. Growth exists outside of your comfort zone. As someone said, "Life is not measured by the number of breaths we take, but by the moments that take our breath away."

> "Do one thing every day that scares you."
> —ELEANOR ROOSEVELT

5. Don't Make Money Your Purpose

Everywhere you look, there are millions of ways to make money. Making money is not a purpose, but rather a by-product of purpose. Develop a career of choice. Find, develop, and hone in on your skills. Find love in what you do, and monetize it by delivering value to others.

Since money is nothing but the exchange of value, we need to increase the value of services. The universal law and philosophy in monetizing the value we add to people's lives can best be described as the following: If you want $10, simply make someone else $100. You will receive 10 percent of what you create for others. If you want to make $100 million, you will need to create and add $1 billion of value.

6. Write Down Your Goals

In a study performed graduate students were asked, "Have you set clear, written goals for your future and made plans to accomplish them?" Eighty-four percent of students had no goals at all, 13 percent had goals but they weren't in writing, and only 3 percent had written goals and plans.

Ten years later, the same group was interviewed again and the results were mind-blowing. The 13 percent of the class who had goals but did not write them down were earning twice the amount of the 84 percent who had no goals. The 3 percent who had written goals were earning, on average, ten times as much as the other 97 percent of the class combined!

7. Dream Big, Act Small

Create a big, inspiring vision of your ideal life—bigger than what you currently know how to accomplish. Then take baby steps today and every day for as many years as it takes to achieve that vision. Small, consistent action is the key to unleashing your power and greatness. The past will never be an indication of your immediate future. The present moment is all that matters. Make your vision bigger than your problems and complaints.

> "I dream my painting, and then I paint my dream."
> —VINCENT VAN GOGH

Dream your purpose. Choose what you intend to do with your gifts. Write down your goals and pursue them relentlessly. Live on purpose and come alive.

> "When you walk with purpose, you collide with destiny."
> —BERTICE BERRY

CHAPTER 27

FREEDOM FROM YES—CREATING CHOICE

W e live in an opportunity-driven culture. So many of us jump from one opportunity to the next. We're always in search of that next big thing. We are haunted by "FOMO," the fear of missing out. We hear inspirational quotes like, "The fun is always on the other side of a yes."

For people stuck in fear, learning to say yes may be an important step in their progression. But for 5 Day Weekenders, it's actually more important to learn how to say no. Yes can hold you captive and prevent you from really breaking free from your limitations. The tyranny of yes is accepting too many opportunities and allowing too many distractions. Never being able to focus on your purpose and the best opportunities often leads to feeling overwhelmed and burned out.

Yes Can Confine You, No Can Free You

For purpose-driven people, no can actually be much more powerful than yes. No keeps your options free and gives you the choice to say yes to and focus on very selective opportunities that are aligned with your purpose, passions, and gifts. No clears out the clutter of life and makes anything you say yes to much more focused, powerful, and enjoyable. The more you say yes, the fewer options you have.

Success depends on your ability to recognize distractions, stay on track, and remain true to yourself. When you don't say no to distractions that have nothing to do with your immediate goals, you become emotionally obligated and overwhelmed with requests to perform for others.

> **"Saying yes to everything will kill you slowly and softly."**
> —STEPHANIE MELISH

In the 5 Day Weekend, we create freedom from the tyranny of yes and expand our ability to choose. We eliminate distractions. We stop being scattered and, instead, focus intently and diligently for a sufficient amount of time to experience real results.

Say No to Distractions

1. Be Clear on Your Core Yes

The Latin word *incido* means "to cut" and is the base of the words incision, excision, and decision. Incision means to cut into something, excision means

> Saying no is not confining, but rather freeing.

to cut out something, and decision means to cut off something. Every time you make a decision you are cutting off possible options, which is why people struggle with making decisions.

The way to get over this struggle is to be super clear on your yes, or your purpose. Understand that saying no to everything else isn't a negative thing; it's how you choose your purpose powerfully.

2. Live from Abundance

We often live from a scarcity mentality, fearful of missing out on opportunities, worried that we won't have enough money or resources. We compare ourselves to others and feel envious when other people succeed. In this mindset, we easily fall into the trap of saying yes too often and to the wrong things.

It takes an abundance mindset to say no. We must trust in our purpose and trust that we will be taken care of when we focus.

3. Remember the "HELL YEAH" Philosophy

Popular TED speaker Derek Sivers teaches a simple philosophy: "If you're not saying, 'HELL YEAH!' to something, then say no." Never commit to anything that doesn't inspire a "HELL YEAH!" Being somewhat interested is a definite no.

4. Value Your Time

Put yourself as the number one priority in your life. When you do, saying no to distractions becomes a powerful drive towards designing your ideal life.

This isn't selfish. It's only by putting yourself first and developing your gifts that you can create the most value for others. Increase your net worth by increasing your value to the rest of the world.

5. Eliminate Disruptions

We have been programmed to be available 24/7 via devices and social media, and to respond to everything immediately. Turn off all notifications in your digital environment for specified periods during the day. Learn to say no to people who try to distract you. Create a schedule and invite people to set appointments with you instead of trying to talk to you whenever they feel like it.

6. Create Daily Productivity Rituals

Here are a few of the daily rituals I use that I recommend you use as well:

- Ensure you have caller ID. Only answer cell phone calls from people you know. Your cell phone is a digital leash. Do not set up voicemail, as it is time disruptive. People who know you will text or email.
- Escape the tyranny of the email inbox. Email less often. The more emails you write, the more you'll receive. Never just check email. Only open your emails if you're committed to answering them. Avoid long-winded emails when you can simply call someone. Use filters to get rid of spam. View your email inbox two to four times a day and run through everything then. Email is a reactive environment, and you can easily fall prey to other people's agendas. Do not view your email inbox in the first one hour of your morning as it may disorientate you from your priorities for the day. Similarly, you should apply a one-hour email detox before you sleep so as to not impact the quality of your sleep in the event of any potential negative news. I recommend a twenty-four-hour email detox every Sunday to aerate and ventilate your mind and body.

> **"The difference between successful people and very successful people is that very successful people say 'no' to almost everything."**
> —WARREN BUFFETT

- Stop watching brain-numbing TV, and only watch TV sparingly. There are no refunds on the time wasted on pointless TV shows.
- Use all your drive time to fill your mind with inspiration and business knowledge. Listen to podcasts. The same goes when you are working out in the gym. During long flights, load up two or three audiobooks on your smartphone.
- Monitor your productivity performance by focusing on an outcome, not the activity. Don't use "to-do" lists.
- Apply the 365 days, 365 hours rule: Wake up one hour earlier than usual each day for one year and work on what you are most passionate about. The dedication of the 365 hours toward your goals will manifest significant results.

7. Be Aware of the Tendency to Please Others

> Avoid the noise of life that erodes your most precious moments.

We often say yes to please others, or because we don't want to let them down. Remember, the more you say yes to someone else's agenda, the more you're saying no to your own. Don't become emotionally oversubscribed to other people's agendas. Opt out of other people's agendas and opt into your own.

Just Say No!

Saying no to the demands of others and to the wrong opportunities—and saying yes to only those things that inspire you—is how you create space to live your ideal life. Otherwise, you become a puppet, pulled by the strings of other people's agendas. Life is short; just say no to distractions.

> "Your time is limited, so don't waste it living someone else's life."
> —STEVE JOBS

CHAPTER 28

FREEDOM FROM FREEDOM FROM PERFECTION— CREATING PRODUCTIVITY

In early 1970, a man named Muhammad was a Bangladeshi economist at Chittagong University. After a devastating cyclone, a bloody war of independence with Pakistan, and severe famine, Bangladesh was suffering deeply. Muhammad was heartbroken over the poverty he saw, realizing his academic economics were doing nothing to alleviate it.

In 1974 he visited a village to learn directly from the people how to help.

He discovered that women creating handcrafts were paying local moneylenders interest rates as high as 10 percent per week. He began loaning money to these women from his own pocket, starting with just $27.

From that initial $27 investment, Nobel Prize–winner Muhammad Yunus built Grameen Bank, which today has 2,565 branches with 22,124 staff serving 8.35 million borrowers (97 percent women) in 81,379 villages. This microcredit pioneer lends out more than a billion dollars a year in loans averaging less than $200.[23] The bank has lifted millions of illiterate peasants out of the depths of poverty by helping them create small but thriving businesses.

> "If we wait until we're ready, we'll be waiting for the rest of our lives."
>
> —LEMONY SNICKET

Imagine what would have happened—or rather, what would *not* have happened—had Muhammad not taken action immediately. Imagine if he had overanalyzed, dawdled over a business plan, waited until he could get investors on board, or waited until the stars were aligned and everything was just perfect. In that case, Grameen Bank never would have launched, and millions of people would have suffered as a result.

Never Let Perfectionism Hold Productivity Hostage

Few things hold back would-be entrepreneurs more than the misguided and delusional idea of perfection. The plain truth is this: entrepreneurship is messy. Conditions will *never* be perfect. Your product or service will never be perfect. Your business systems will constantly be in need of improvement.

5 Day Weekenders don't sit around talking about all their great ideas while never taking action to execute any of them. They act. They do. They produce. They ship products out the door, repeatedly and incessantly. They develop a tolerance for imperfect and incomplete. They understand that failure only exists if they give up; otherwise, it's a course correction. They know that problems exist to teach us lessons, as long as our vision is greater than our problems. Productivity, they've learned, comes from initiating and working hard in the trenches, not nitpicking and hiding in the lab. In life we never lose—we either win or we learn a valuable lesson.

Conquer Perfectionism — Boost Productivity

1. Embrace Failure

The greatest barrier to success is the fear of failure. Successful entrepreneurs fail quickly and often, knowing it's precisely what gets them closer to success. Frequent failure means you're

"Success is stumbling from failure to failure with no loss of enthusiasm."
—WINSTON CHURCHILL

acting. If you keep going forward — and learn the right lessons from your failures — success is inevitable. Failure is just a resting place. It is an opportunity to begin again more intelligently.

2. Set Deadlines — and Stick to Them

There's no shortage of business ideas and opportunities. Pick one. Commit to it. Figure out the steps you need to take to launch the idea. Then set deadlines for completing each step and achieving specific milestones. Your most important deadline is your launch date.

3. Use Accountability Partners and Techniques

Ask people to become your accountability partners and hold you accountable to your deadlines. One effective technique is to commit to donating a sizeable amount of money to a cause you don't like if you don't meet your deadlines.

Launch your business by your deadline even, and especially, if it's not perfect. You can always improve it over time, but no progress will happen until you actually ship.

4. Learn to Adjust Quickly

If something isn't working, it's time to take a long, hard look at your processes and systems to discover what's broken. It's not enough to work hard — you must also work smart.

Ship quickly and often, but then immediately adjust to market feedback. Experiment, test, and measure your results. Fine-tune your offer and systems over time.

5. Replace Perfectionism with Excellence

It's a fine ideal to want to strive for the best quality in everything you produce. But holding to a standard of perfection can do more harm than good. Instead of striving for perfection, strive for excellence. Keep improving, but don't reject something because it's less than perfect. Done is better than perfect.

> **"Perfection is the enemy of done."**
> —ANDREA SCHER

Start Now!

The best advice I could give anyone who longs for the 5 Day Weekend but isn't sure where to start is this: Stop waiting and start something—*anything*. You will never have enough knowledge or skill or confidence. There will never be a better time than right now.

Waiting until you feel ready, trying to do everything just perfectly, is precisely how you stay stuck and never progress. You're ready just as you are. The time is now. Eager productivity always trumps hesitant perfectionism.

> **"Striving for perfection is the greatest stopper there is. It's your excuse to yourself for not doing anything. Instead, strive for excellence, doing your best."**
> —LAURENCE OLIVIER

CHAPTER 29

FREEDOM FROM STUFF, CREATING SIMPLICITY

Henry was born into a modest New England family in Concord, Massachusetts. His father owned and operated a pencil factory, and his mother rented out rooms in the family's home to boarders.

He was a bright student and was accepted into Harvard, where he excelled. Upon graduating, he had received the most prestigious education. He was smart and driven. His father was a successful businessman. He could have followed in his father's footsteps, or pursued a distinguished career in law or medicine. All the stars had aligned for him to live the "good life" of luxury.

But something nagged at him. He felt as if there was something more than the conventional path society was pushing him into. He wasn't content with following the crowd. He returned home and began working in his father's factory while pondering his life path. Restlessness continued to plague him.

After working for a couple of years, he determined to embark on an experiment to live alone in the woods. "I went to the woods," he said, "because I wished to live deliberately, to front only the essential facts of life, and see if I could not learn what it had to teach, and not, when I came to die, discover that I had not lived."

Henry David Thoreau walked away from a life of privilege and lived alone on the shores of Walden Pond. From his two-year experiment emerged his book *Walden*, one of the greatest classics in American literature and the bible for simple living.

He wrote of observing people who had the "misfortune" of being born into wealth and being "crushed and smothered" under the load of lands and assets to care for. He concluded that, "Most of the luxuries, and many of the so-called comforts of life, are not only not indispensable, but positive hindrances to the elevation of mankind."

I couldn't agree with him more.

Materialism Does Not Create Happiness

Wealth gives you the freedom to purchase nice material things, if that's what you really want. There's certainly nothing wrong with that, and everyone values different things. However, I would caution you against thinking that's what gives you "the good life." What good does it do to achieve the 5 Day Weekend lifestyle on paper, and yet still be tied down by liabilities, stress, and hassle?

The good life is found in simplicity—the simplicity of meaningful relationships, unforgettable experiences, the freedom to simply be in the moment without worrying about bills and managing your stuff.

Create More Simplicity and Happiness

1. Understand That Your Stuff Does Not Define You

A research study in 1988 found "especially striking evidence" in the "diminished sense of self when possessions are unintentionally lost or stolen."[24] You are not your possessions. You can lose all your possessions without losing any essential part of you.

2. Stop Comparing Yourself to Others

One study found that money only makes people happier if it improves their social rank. The researchers found that simply being highly paid wasn't enough—to be happy, people must perceive themselves as being more highly paid than their friends and work colleagues. Earning $1 million a year appears to be not enough to make you happy if you know your friends all earn $2 million.[25]

> **"Comparison is the thief of joy."**
> —THEODORE ROOSEVELT

Choose to be happy as you are, and with what you have.

3. Stop Trying to Impress People

Much of materialism is simply based on trying to impress people. Stop it. Be real. Be who you are. Live your authentic life without caring what anyone else thinks of you.

4. What Makes You Happy?

Failure is most often defined as not reaching one's goals. But an even deeper sense of failure is achieving inauthentic goals for the wrong reasons. Do you want to be a millionaire to prove to the world how cool you are, or to be free and make a positive difference?

> **"Americanism: Using money you haven't earned to buy things you don't need to impress people you don't like."**
> —ROBERT QUILLEN

What does success look like for you? What would be your ideal life? What makes you happy? Forget what the world says and what everyone else is pursuing. Pursue *your* version of authentic success.

5. Cultivate Gratitude and Presence

The saying "The best things in life are free" really is true. There's no house, car, or other possession that can ever rival watching a sunrise or eating a peach. Cultivate an attitude of gratitude. Never take anything for granted. Revel in each moment of every day. See the gifts and beauty in everything around you.

6. Limit Your Exposure to Advertising

Advertisers have perfected the art of making us buy things to reinforce our self-identity. We feel superior when we have stuff other people don't have, and vice versa. Stop buying into the message that you're not good enough. Stop buying things to "improve" who you are. Because ultimately, no product is going to make you a better version of you.

> "We don't need more to be thankful for, we just need to be more thankful."
> —CARLOS CASTANEDA

To help with this, limit your exposure to media and advertising. Watch less TV. Use TiVo or services such as Netflix, Hulu, or Amazon to watch your favorite programs on demand without commercials. Listen to audiobooks while you're driving instead of listening to mundane radio. Maintain your insatiable desire to educate yourself on relevant topics. Reading insightful material is like downloading new software to your brain.

7. Purge Your Clutter Every Six Months

Every six months, go through your house and get rid of everything you haven't used or no longer need. Do it in small chunks, one room at a time. The same goes for your garage; get rid of anything that does not look like a car and donate it to charity.

Make quick and merciless decisions — if you're on the fence about something, let it go. Be mindful of your emotions if you struggle with getting rid of things. Do you find yourself clinging? Why?

"Many wealthy people are little more than janitors of their possessions."

—FRANK LLOYD WRIGHT

Ignore the Joneses

News flash: The Joneses aren't any happier than you. Stop trying to keep up with them and, instead, live your authentic life.

Money won't make you happy — if you're miserable without it, you'll be even more miserable with it. Choose simplicity and be happy. Use your riches to create freedom for yourself and make a difference for others, rather than to impress people or accumulate stuff.

"Our greatest fear should not be that we won't succeed, but that we will succeed at something that doesn't matter."

—D. L. MOODY

CHAPTER 30

FREEDOM FROM FREEDOM—CREATING ADVENTURE

L arry is sitting in his backyard in a lawn chair. Drinking beer. Bored with his job as a truck driver. Frustrated in his dream of becoming an air force pilot because of his poor eyesight.

So he decides to do something about it. He gets helium tanks and forty-five weather balloons. He fills up the balloons and attaches them to his lawn chair. He packs a pellet pistol, a parachute, a CB radio, and some sandwiches and beer. He dubs the craft "Inspiration I," straps himself into the chair, and cuts the moorings loose.

Larry rises into the air. Fast. He'd expected to level off at thirty feet, but he rises a thousand feet per minute and doesn't level off until he hits more than 15,000 feet. His plan was to use the pellet gun to shoot balloons to control his descent, but now he's too afraid.

He starts drifting into the flight path of incoming planes to Long Beach (California) Airport. Worried, he uses his CB radio to transmit a mayday call. Operators at the airport receive his call and maintain contact with him.

Larry continues drifting. Eventually, he shoots out several balloons. He begins descending slowly. Ninety minutes after lift-off he lands on the ground, where he is met by police officers.

When a reporter asks him why he'd done something so stupid, Larry Walters replies, "A man can't just sit around."

> "Dream as if you'll live forever. Live as if you'll die today."
> —JAMES DEAN

It's a true story. It happened on July 2, 1982. And what he said is true as well. I don't recommend you fill balloons and fly in a lawn chair, but I do recommend that you fill your life with adventure.

Wealth Is About Challenge

In a survey of North American youth performed by the National Center on Addiction and Substance Abuse in 2003, 91 percent of respondents reported that they regularly experience boredom.[26]

How is it possible that so many people are bored in the wealthiest nation in the world with so much opportunity? One answer is found in other research, which shows that boredom is accompanied by a lack of challenge and meaning. All too often, people pursue wealth simply because they want more comfort and security. And when they become wealthy and life is easy, they lose their zest for life.

5 Day Weekenders have a completely different orientation to wealth. They don't crave mere comfort alone; they crave adventure and experiential living—whatever that means to them personally. They suck the marrow out of life. The process of becoming wealthy is a grand adventure for them, and they use their wealth to fuel more adventures. Happiness increases with wealth—if you use it to increase experiences.

There is a science to generating money, but there is definitely an art to creating fulfillment. Success without fulfillment is the ultimate failure. 5 Day Weekenders never rest on their laurels, but rather continue pushing the boundaries of achievement throughout their lives. They don't want to be the richest person in the graveyard.

> "A ship in harbor is safe, but that is not what ships are built for."
>
> —J. A. SHEDD

Fight Boredom and Create Adventure

1. Put Wealth in Its Proper Perspective

The American Psychological Association reports that "...when people organize their lives around the pursuit of wealth, their happiness can actually decrease.... Individuals who say that goals for money, image, and popularity are relatively important to them also report less satisfaction in life, fewer experiences of pleasant emotions, and more depression and anxiety."[27]

The 5 Day Weekend isn't simply about being rich for its own sake, but rather about maximizing your contribution and taking full advantage of this short life.

2. Create Your List of Major Life Goals

Write down all the goals you want to achieve, dreams you want to fulfill, and experiences you want to have throughout your lifetime. Take time to create a list that really inspires you. Dream big! Nothing is too outlandish. Explore the movie viewfinder of your mind. Emotionalize and socialize your goals. Imprint and internalize them on a cellular level. Have your peers hold you accountable, and cut off every sign of retreat in order to give yourself permission to succeed. You have to fight for your dreams; otherwise unfulfilled dreams have a habit of haunting you for the rest of your life.

3. Never Stop Setting Goals

Once you achieve goals, keep setting new ones. Never stop raising the bar on yourself.

4. Expand Your Hobbies and Skills

Ever wanted to learn how to play the guitar, learn how to dance, or learn how to code an app? What are you waiting for?

5. Get into Mindfulness

Jon Kabat-Zinn, one of the most popular mindfulness teachers in the West, defines mindfulness as "paying attention in a particular way: on purpose, in the present moment, and non-judgmentally."[28] It's formally practiced through meditation. Mindfulness has been proven in countless studies to improve your mental and physical health and overall well-being. It makes you more grateful and more present in all of life. It enables you to see the beauty and wonder in each moment. In short, it's an extremely effective method for fighting boredom.

> "If your life's work can be accomplished in your lifetime, you're not thinking big enough."
> —WES JACKSON

6. Change Your Friends

Consider the priorities of your friends. Are they simply pursuing material wealth, comfort, and security, or are they fully engaged with life? Is it time for a change? Set the parameters as to whom you invite into your life.

7. Be Unreasonable

We tend to be so reasonable and conservative in life. Perhaps it's time to break out of that mold. Move to another country. Ride a bike across the country. Live alone in the woods for two months. Do *anything* other than sit around complaining about feeling bored.

Carpe Diem!

Today, we have more opportunities than kings in the past could have ever dreamed of. Life is an unrepeatable gift. There are no do-overs. Live fully and experience the magic that happens outside of your comfort zone. Don't choose to live a life that craves routine, familiarity, order, and predictability. Never take anything for granted. Seize the day and make your life a nonstop adventure. You can't just sit around and expect to be excited about life. Enjoy the ride of your life and unleash your best work each and every day.

> "Life should not be a journey to the grave with the intention of arriving safely in a pretty and well preserved body, but rather to skid in broadside in a cloud of smoke, thoroughly used up, totally worn out, and loudly proclaiming 'Wow! What a Ride!'"
> —HUNTER S. THOMPSON

CHAPTER 31

FREEDOM FROM REGRET—CREATING PEACE

Karl Pillemer is an American gerontologist who studies the changes people experience as they age. Bronnie Ware is an Australian nurse who cares for people in the last few weeks of their lives. They both realized they were sitting on a gold mine of knowledge that could be learned from people who have gone before us and experienced it all. They each took a bit different approach to mine this wealth of elderly advice, and the results of their studies are incredibly valuable.

Karl asked more than 1,200 seniors, "Over the course of your life, what are the most important lessons you would like to pass on to younger people?" From those responses he wrote his book, *30 Lessons for Living: Tried and True Advice from the Wisest Americans.* Here are the top ten responses that emerged:

1. Choose a career for the intrinsic rewards, not the financial ones.
2. Act now like you will need your body for a hundred years.
3. Take a risk and a leap of faith when opportunity knocks.
4. Choose a mate with extreme care.
5. Travel more.
6. Don't wait to say words that need to be said, such as "I'm sorry," "Thank you," "I love you."
7. Time is of the essence: Live as though life is short — because it is.
8. Happiness is a choice, not a condition.
9. Time spent worrying is time wasted: Stop worrying.
10. When it comes to making the most of your life, think small. Savor the simple daily pleasures.

Bronnie interviewed her patients and asked them what they regretted most about their lives. The most common responses she received, which she expounds on in her book *The Top Five Regrets of the Dying*, were:

1. "I wish I'd had the courage to live a life true to myself, not the life others expected of me."
2. "I wish I hadn't worked so hard."
3. "I wish I'd had the courage to express my feelings."
4. "I wish I had stayed in touch with my friends."
5. "I wish I had let myself be happier."

These responses are worth pondering deeply.

Live Without Regret

No one wants to lie on their deathbed plagued by all the things they wish they had done, said, and experienced. Yet sadly, we all live as if we have forever. We run from the inevitable reality that we're going to die and fill our time with avoidant work, petty distractions, and meaningless entertainment. Death is non-negotiable but the quality of your life is negotiable. How you live it and whom you spend it with is negotiable. Make your stand now. Make a declaration as to the quality of your life.

The 5 Day Weekend lifestyle is about replacing all these with important contributions, purposeful adventure, and meaningful service. It should be wild and unpredictable, with the operating methodology of taking calculated risks. It's your private undertaking, a spiritual journey, and an act of rebirth.

Ways to Create Peace

1. Begin with the End in Mind

Imagine that you're able to attend your own funeral. What would you want people to say about you? What do you want to have accomplished? How do you want to be remembered?

Use that exercise to write your personal mission statement— your plan for success that clearly defines who you want to be and what you want to do. Read your mission statement daily.

2. Be Authentic

Don't live other people's dreams. Get crystal clear on who you really are, what drives you, what you love, what you want to accomplish. Stay true to yourself no matter what. Live by design, not by default. Hell on earth is meeting the person you could have been.

> "If the ladder is not leaning against the right wall, every step we take just gets us to the wrong place faster."
> —STEPHEN R. COVEY

3. Use the "Deathbed Test" to Make Decisions

When faced with important decisions, ask yourself which path you'll regret taking on your deathbed. Then take the other path—particularly if it scares you to death.

4. Stand Up for Yourself

Don't be a passive observer who lets life pass you by. Be an active participant. Don't be afraid to ruffle feathers and stand up for yourself; if you don't do it, no one else will. It feels scary and risky sometimes, but taking that risk is far better than the alternative — the guaranteed disappointment of not getting what you want. Break some rules, forgive quickly, laugh uncontrollably, and never regret anything that made you smile.

5. Stop Worrying

Worrying accomplishes nothing, other than contributing to health problems. The only outcome it affects is your happiness in the present moment. Happiness is a choice. It's not dependent on external circumstances working out just as you expect them to. Choose to be happy no matter what happens. Smile your way through tough times. This lesson will serve you well. Smile and laugh. It's the shock absorber and lubricant of your life.

> Smile, it bends the universe.

6. Remember, *Everything* Is Fixable

In 2003 *The New Yorker* magazine published an article about the suicide capital of the world, San Francisco's Golden Gate Bridge.[29] The article featured thoughts from the small percentage of people who had survived the jump. Most of these people reported feeling instant regret the moment they stepped off the bridge. As one young man put it, "I instantly realized that everything in my life that I'd thought was unfixable was totally fixable — except for having just jumped."[30]

No matter how bad life may seem, no matter how much you think you've screwed up, no matter how afraid you've been in the past — *everything* can be changed with bold action. Don't wait. If there's something about your life you don't like, change it. Every day should be a New Year's Resolution. Live without regret and never look back. Stop living in the past.

7. Take Charge of Your Schedule

How are you spending your time on a daily basis? Are your daily activities aligned with your personal mission statement?

There will never be a better time than right now to own your schedule. Regrets don't develop from major mistakes, but rather from the tiny, seemingly inconsequential moments that pass you by every day. Regret isn't a dramatic avalanche, but rather an imperceptible erosion. Most people are so busy making a living that they forget to live.

> "What surprises me most is man, because he sacrifices his health in order to make money. Then he sacrifices money to recuperate his health. And then he is so anxious about the future that he doesn't enjoy the present; the result being he doesn't live in the present or the future. He lives as if he's never going to die, and then he dies having never really lived."
>
> —DALAI LAMA

Live Like You're Dying

Tim McGraw's country song "Live Like You Were Dying" talks about a man diagnosed with something serious, which forces him to reconsider how he's living his life. Facing the inevitability of death, he rearranges his priorities and starts living more freely and adventurously.

It's a strange song, honestly—because who isn't dying? We don't need a terminal diagnosis to tell us that. Our days are finite. One day, they will indeed run out. The death rate is 100 percent. Live like you were dying. Because you are.

> **"It's better to look ahead and prepare than to look back and regret."**
> —JACKIE JOYNER-KERSEE

CHAPTER 32

FREEDOM FROM SELF — CREATING GENEROSITY

Consider two possible scenarios. Tell me which of them you would prefer, and which of them you think will make you happier. The first is winning the lottery. The second is getting paralyzed and becoming a paraplegic.

It seems obvious, right? Fascinatingly, the research turns the obvious on its head. Studies have proven that one year after losing the use of their legs, and a year after winning the lotto, lottery winners and paraplegics are equally happy with their lives.

From studies like this, psychologists have created the term "impact bias," referring to the tendency to overestimate the hedonic impact of future events. In other words, we far overestimate the happiness, satisfaction, and contentment we'll experience when we become rich and famous. It's empirically not true that more money will make you happier.

But you know what *has* been proven to make you happier? Service and generosity. Dozens of studies have shown that helping others, donating to charity, and doing volunteer work provides the following benefits[31]:

1. It makes you feel good. Psychologists refer to the feel-good chemicals released in your body as the "helper's high."
2. It boosts your self-esteem and overall well-being.
3. It improves your friendships, strengthens your social connectedness, and reduces feelings of isolation and loneliness.
4. It boosts your mood and makes you more positive and optimistic.
5. It makes you feel more rewarded, fulfilled, and empowered and enriches your sense of purpose.
6. It lowers your stress and makes you more calm and peaceful.
7. It makes you more grateful for what you have.
8. It strengthens you psychologically and gives you a greater ability to bounce back after experiencing challenges and negative moods.

The Secret to Happiness

Psychoanalyst Manfred Kets de Vries is a therapist who treats the ultra rich, whom he says suffer from "Wealth Fatigue Syndrome." He says, "For the super-rich, houses, yachts, cars and planes are like new toys that they play with for five minutes and then lose interest in. Pretty soon, to attain the same buzz they have to spend more money. All the spending is a mad attempt to cover up boredom and depression."[32]

> "Making money is a happiness; making other people happy is a superhappiness."
> —MUHAMMAD YUNUS

What all of us need to feel more fulfilled and happy isn't more toys, but rather more meaning through service. Wake up each day inspired to contribute to something bigger than yourself.

There is a Chinese saying that goes, "If you want happiness for an hour, take a nap. If you want happiness for a day, go fishing. If you want happiness for a year, inherit a fortune. If you want happiness for a lifetime, help somebody." Our greatest sages have suggested the same thing for centuries: Happiness is found in helping others.

Generosity Creates Meaning

1. Help People Who Are Struggling

We often gravitate toward selfishness, not because that's our true nature, but because we simply get trapped in the grind of work and daily routines. We don't see how other people are struggling because we're just not looking.

Be more conscious about seeing the pain felt and challenges experienced by others. In simply seeing them, you will be much more likely to act.

> "He who lives only to benefit himself confers on the world a benefit when he dies."
> —TERTULLIAN

2. Travel More

A simple and extremely effective way to get outside your own bubble is to travel. Go see how other people live. Don't just watch it on TV—experience it for yourself. Changing your environment is a great way to change your perspective, and therefore your behavior.

Traverse the planet, jettison your comfort zone, and immerse yourself in exotic cultures and cuisines. The more you travel the richer you become. As a teenager, traveling became a new part of my life, and I've developed many valuable lessons along the way. You never return the way you left.

3. Choose a Cause to Support

Instead of just giving randomly, consider finding a cause that can become a lifelong passion for you. For example, promoting cancer research, funding an orphanage, saving children from sex trafficking, or helping villages in developing countries get clean water. What speaks to your heart? Where do you really want to make a difference? You may even be inspired to start your own charitable foundation.

Building businesses, making money, and having adventures are all important, fun, and rewarding. But ultimately, as research shows, the greatest meaning and fulfillment in life are found in what we contribute to others.

> **"What you leave behind is not what is engraved in stone monuments, but what is woven into the lives of others."**
> —PERICLES

Call to Action
Your Freedom Lifestyle Plan

Live on Purpose

What is your life's purpose? What do you want to be remembered for? What contribution do you want to make to humanity?

Create More Choice

What activities drain your energy and distract you from your true purpose? What's your plan for eliminating these?

Increase Your Productivity

What projects are holding you hostage because of perfectionism? What's your plan for starting and launching them?

Live with More Simplicity

Go through your home and do a formal "purge." Get rid of anything you haven't used in six months.

Choose Adventure

Write down your "Bucket List," the most inspiring, challenging, or just plain fun things you want to accomplish before you die.

Create Peace

Imagine that you're able to attend your own funeral. What would you want people to say about you? What do you want to have accomplished? How do you want to be remembered?

Write your personal mission statement—your plan for success that clearly defines who you want to be and what you want to do.

Find Meaning Through Generosity

Research and choose a charity that aligns with your passions and purpose. Commit to donating a percentage of your income.

 Go to our website to download and print this worksheet at 5DayWeekend.com.
Code: P15

As a child, you used to dream. Your mind wasn't shackled by logic, false beliefs, or societal limitations. Everything was possible, and the world was wondrous and magical.

Then, as you aged, you started developing false and limiting beliefs about yourself and the world around you. You started buying into societal programming. When people told you something wasn't possible, you believed them. When your peers chose jobs and careers based on their own internal limitations, you followed suit. You started thinking more "responsibly" and "sensibly." And in this process, the flame of your dreams died down to mere embers, and in some cases may have been entirely extinguished.

My invitation to you is to breathe life into your dreams again. Cast off the shackles of your false beliefs and societal programming. Realize that the vast majority of your limitations are only in your mind.

What would you do if money was no longer the primary reason for doing or not doing something? What grand adventures would you live? What noble causes would you champion? What great feats would you accomplish?

All these things are made possible by your 5 Day Weekend. Achieve your 5 Day Weekend, and your dreams will follow....

CHAPTERS

- **Escape the Ordinary**

- **Build Your Own 5 Day Weekend**

- *Call to Action*

  Your 5 Day Weekend Plan Contract

CHAPTER 33

ESCAPE THE ORDINARY

I was born with a poor biological template. I developed chronic allergies, debilitating asthma, and I was nearsighted. I was medically confined to my bedroom for the first decade of my life.

When I was eight years old, a traveling salesman knocked on our front door in Port Melbourne, Australia, and sold my non-English speaking parents a set of the *Encyclopedia Britannica*. That set turned out to be one of the greatest influences on my life. It was the spark and secret kindling that set my imagination on fire. My imagination had stretched my mind, and it would never retract to its original dimensions.

I read the encyclopedia constantly and, without my parents knowing, I'd take it to bed with me. I'd shine a flashlight under the sheets, flick the pages of a volume through to a subject that fascinated me, and read until I nodded off to sleep. Sometimes I'd stay awake past midnight, dreaming about the things I was going to pursue in life, and imagining the world that was out there waiting for me.

Growing up, an inspirational character for me was the comic book adventurer named Tintin. Tintin was living the "never grow up" dream, and I traveled the world through his pages, taking in every exotic detail. I read and reread Tintin books in our school library, daydreaming about his magical life. In his various adventures he was a pilot, space explorer, mountain climber, and deep-sea diver. He also climbed the mountains of Nepal, rescued African slaves, battled pirates, and dived down to the deepest abyss of the ocean to explore shipwrecks.

Nik writes his list of life goals.
8 down, 2 to go.

1. To walk on the moon.
2. To go to the space station on a rocket and live there.
3. To become an Astronaut.
4. To own Beautiful Places all over the world.
5. To travel and Explore more than 100 countries.
6. To go to the bottom of the Ocean and have lunch on the Titanic.
7. To become a mountain climber and Climb the highest mountains in the world.
8. To run with the bulls in Spain.
9. To become a millionaire.
10. To become a Rock 'n Roll star

When I reflect back on the adventures of Tintin, I realize that my childhood dreams have come true. Many times in the course of my adventures, I've been in some far-flung destination and had a weird feeling of déjà vu—a Tintin flashback.

I was fascinated by space travel. Growing up, I was glued to the TV, watching the U.S. and Russian launches. This was *the* big deal then. All this adventure fueled my desire to get in a rocket ship and go myself.

Writing the Script of My Life

The encyclopedia, the lure of space travel, and the Tintin adventures opened up all the things I wanted to accomplish. I sat down and wrote my highest aspirations in life.

I drafted my own screenplay of goals. I was the actor, the producer, and the director. Here I am as an eight-year-old, with my list of ten life goals. Pretty ambitious. Dreaming and thinking big. It has fueled my life ever since.

Since writing down that list at age eight, I've accomplished almost everything on the list. I have two major goals remaining: rocketing to a space station orbiting 250 miles above the Earth, and walking on the moon. Even those goals are within my reach.

My Adventures

I became the first flight-qualified, certified civilian astronaut from Australia, and was a backup astronaut for the TMA 13 NASA/Russian space mission. I remain in mission allocation status for a future space flight to the International Space Station.

For a few years I lived in Moscow, and I graduated from the Yuri Gagarin Cosmonaut Training Center in Star City. During the Communist era, Soviet cosmonauts were quietly chosen, groomed, and trained behind a veil of secrecy.

Zero Gravity Training

My life has been filled with extreme adventures. I have visited over 149 countries. I have trekked with the Tuareg Bedouins across the Sahara Desert. I broke the sound barrier in a modified Russian MIG 25 supersonic interceptor jet, traveling at almost Mach 3.2 (2,170 mph, 3,470 kmh), and viewed the curvature of the earth. My rock band performed and toured with big names like Bon Jovi and Deep Purple. I dived down five miles deep in a pressurized biosphere to have lunch on the bow of the shipwreck RMS *Titanic* in the North Atlantic Ocean.

I have climbed the highest peaks of five continents, including the mighty Mt. Aconcagua in the Andes. I have two more peaks to summit on my attempt to become one of a handful of climbers in history who have climbed the Seven Summits—the highest

mountains of all seven of the world's continents. I did a Navy Seals HALO skydive jump with oxygen, above the summit of Mt. Everest in Nepal at over 30,000 feet, on my most recent birthday.

I have rappelled into the heart of the most active volcanoes in the world. I

Peak of Mt. Aconcagua, Andes, 22,841 feet

have storm-chased tornadoes in the Midwest and hurricanes across the Atlantic Ocean. I even negotiated with the former deposed dictator of Egypt to spend a night in the nearly 5,000-year-old Cheops Pyramid in Giza, Egypt. I spent the night alone in the King's Chamber of the pyramid and slept in the sarcophagus in total darkness. The very same sarcophagus that Napoleon Bonaparte, Alexander the Great, Herodotus, Sir Isaac Newton, and other giants of history had slept in. Media outlets dubbed me the "Thrillionaire."

My Worldwide Business

Over the last two decades, my companies have impacted over one million people in more than fifty-seven countries. I deliver keynote speeches and facilitate entrepreneurial training courses around the world. I even get the opportunity to speak in remote locations most foreigners would simply never visit. Just recently, I spoke in the communist "hermit kingdom" of North Korea and taught geography to a classroom

"Do not go where the path may lead, go instead where there is no path and leave a trail."
—RALPH WALDO EMERSON

of teenagers about to graduate. I have conducted an entrepreneurial mastermind seminar to more than 750 investors and business owners in Tehran, Iran.

It's Time to Live *Your* Dreams

My adventurous life has not happened because I was born into wealth. Lacking a wealthy friend such as Tintin's Captain Haddock, I realized that if I wanted to become an adventurer like Tintin, I would need to develop multiple pillars of income in order to afford such a lifestyle. I wasn't born rich — but I was born rich in human potential. My life by design was never coincidental or lucky. I have merely acted out the script I created for my life — a screenplay I wrote as a young child. My manifested reality was the result of every decision made in my life. I did have medical issues earlier in my childhood, but I refused to be held captive by them. I was forced to clear any obstacles that threatened to obstruct my path of self-discovery. I'm no more special than anyone else. I've simply set my sights on big goals and have never stopped working to achieve them.

> "Don't be an extra in your own movie."
> —BOB PROCTOR

There's nothing stopping you from doing the same. You may not care about traveling or anything else I've done. I don't share my life experiences with you because I think you should care about anything I've accomplished, but rather to simply inspire you to live your own version of the ideal life.

There is no shortage of adventures to live and thrills to be experienced. You may want to live on the beach and surf every day. Perhaps you want to go on an epic RV trip. Your dream could be to do frequent humanitarian trips to developing countries. Maybe you just want to spend more time with your family or simply have the leisure time to read more.

Whatever it is for you, go after it. Don't let anyone tell you it's impossible; don't let anything stop you. Life is the greatest show on earth. Ensure you have front-row seats. You have an abundance of opportunities that people in the past could not even have dreamed of. Eliminate all excuses from your mind and vocabulary. Cut off the pessimists and haters in your life. Surround yourself with inspirational people, and immerse yourself in inspirational material. Do whatever it takes to escape the trap of the ordinary.

Because I can promise you this: It is so worth it.

> **"Start by doing what's necessary; then do what's possible; and suddenly you are doing the impossible."**
> —ST. FRANCIS OF ASSISI

CHAPTER 34

BUILD YOUR OWN 5 DAY WEEKEND

In warfare terminology, strategy involves large-scale, long-range planning and development. Tactics deal with the deployment and use of troops in actual combat. In short, strategy is the big-picture stuff. Tactics are the nitty-gritty, in-the-trenches details.

What Garrett and I have given you is the 5 Day Weekend strategy. We can't tell you what tactics you should use, or what your specific, day-to-day plan should look like. Everyone is different. Everyone has different interests, strengths, and opportunities. We've laid out the map. Now you must navigate the territory.

No two 5 Day Weekend plans will look the same. But, in the big picture, here's what they'll all have in common:

1. Obsessive Focus on Freedom

5 Day Weekenders aren't your typical 9-to-5 types. They don't plan on working for someone else for forty years so they can collect a pension check. They don't sell out their dreams for the illusory "security" of a "safe" and comfortable job.

They are warrior-entrepreneurs who are obsessively and relentlessly focused on freedom at all costs. They do whatever it takes, and for as long as it takes, to break free. They will never be satisfied until they are financially free—and even then they don't coast, but rather continue progressively building more freedom.

5 Day Weekenders get back up each time they fall. They learn from their failures and get smarter, wiser, and closer to success each time they fail. They never give up.

2. Thinking Outside the Box

5 Day Weekenders have unplugged from the "Matrix." They see through the lies and vested interests of corporations and the media. They understand the fine print and read between the lines of the social contract. They color outside the lines. They rattle the cages of societal norms.

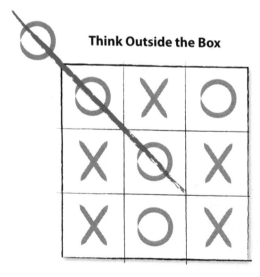

Think Outside the Box

They never do things because "that's the way it's always been done." They live life on their terms. They are mavericks and renegades, pioneers and explorers, creators and innovators. They're constantly looking for ways to do things smarter, better, bigger.

3. Cash Flow Investing — Not Accumulation

5 Day Weekenders don't invest in long-term accumulation vehicles that benefit financial institutions more than them. They
invest in smarter, savvier vehicles that provide immediate and
perpetual cash flow. They don't read *Money* magazine or listen to
popular pundits.

They understand that the path to freedom is cash flow, that
financial independence comes from creating more passive cash
flow than their expenses. And they know they don't have to wait
thirty years to create it.

4. Focused Investing — Not Diversification

5 Day Weekenders don't manage their risk by diversifying. On
the contrary, they manage risk by focusing. They understand that
diversification in mediocre investments is a passive, "hope-and-
pray" strategy for the ignorant.

Although the ultimate goal of 5 Day Weekenders is to create
passive cash flow, they take an active role in the investments they
choose to deliver it. They don't follow the crowd. They research
every investment in great detail. They know exactly what they're
investing in. They know their exit strategy. As a result, they have
much greater control over their investments.

5. Strengths-Based Investing

5 Day Weekenders understand their passions, interests, strengths,
and weaknesses as investors. They focus on the areas where they
have knowledge, skill, and passion. They don't stray into areas
they don't understand or choose something they have no passion for only because it can make them money. They know that
the safest and best way to make money is to focus on what they
do best.

294 PUSH THE BOUNDARIES

5 Day Weekenders are also focused on creating and adding value. Since they know themselves well, they know how they can bring unique value to the table with any investment. They don't just hand their money over to someone and hope for the best. They leverage their unique strengths and skills to improve investments.

6. Living on Purpose

5 Day Weekenders aren't in it just for the money. They understand that money is only a means to the ultimate end of financial freedom. And freedom isn't about lying around on the beach all day every day—it's about living on purpose.

They strive to make the world a better place. The more money they earn, the more impact they contribute with their purpose. Their value is no longer what they know, it is what they share with the world. Financial independence isn't the stopping point for them—it's just the beginning.

Your Next Steps

You've just been given a bunch of information. You have a lot to digest. You have a number of decisions to make. Your 5 Day Weekend plan will be completely unique to you. To start building it, here are your next steps:

1. Commit

Make the commitment now to achieve your 5 Day Weekend. Set a date by which you want to achieve it. Write down your goal. Read it every day. Never give up.

2. Know Yourself

Go on a never-ending journey of self-discovery. Use the tools in this book, and any others you find, to discover your strengths, weaknesses, interests, passions, and purpose. The more you know yourself, the easier it is to choose the right business opportunities and investments, and the more effective you'll be as an entrepreneur and investor.

3. Get Your Financial House in Order

Follow the steps and instructions found in Part I ("Keep More Money") to reduce and ultimately eliminate your debt, plug cash flow leaks, maximize your financial efficiency, begin capturing wealth, establish a healthy financial baseline, and build a foundation for maximizing your production.

4. Map Out Your Plan to Increase Your Entrepreneurial Income

Using the information in this book and other resources, decide which entrepreneurial opportunities you want to pursue to start increasing your income. Brainstorm and research and come up with your own ideas.

5. Take Action

Choose a plan of attack and do it! Don't let your fears, self-doubt, or the discouraging voices of others stop you. Start something. Build something. The best way to learn is through experience. And remember, adjust your plan as you build experience and learn. Maximize your failures by learning the right lessons.

> "Goals in stone, plans in sand."

A picture hanging on the wall of my office shows a mousetrap and a mouse. Most mice walk head on into the trap, flirt with the cheese, and get caught. But the mouse in my picture is different: He is shimmying down a vertical wire to the mousetrap to claim his cheese reward.

This simple picture portrays my life's mantra: Think outside the box. The box of the ordinary 9-to-5 life is a trap. We don't have to walk into that trap. We can escape it—and still get as much cheese as we want. The rules for getting out of your box are written clearly on the outside of the box.

Achieving the 5 Day Weekend lifestyle may seem impossible. It may seem like it's reserved only for a special few. But remember Roger Bannister, the famed English runner who broke the four-minute mile in 1954—a supposedly impossible feat. More interesting than his original feat is the fact that, within nine months of his record, thirty other runners achieved the milestone as well. Impossible is not a fact or declaration but an opinion. Impossible is a temporary state of mind.

The 5 Day Weekend *has* been achieved, not just by me but by thousands of other people across the globe. The record has been broken, the floodgates have been released. Now it's *your* turn.

Accept the challenge. Go to the next page and complete your 5 Day Weekend Plan contract.

> "There is only one success: to be able to spend your life in your own way."
> —CHRISTOPHER MORLEY

Call to Action

Your 5 Day Weekend Plan Contract

I accept the challenge!

I am wholeheartedly committed to achieving my 5 Day Weekend and living my life to its fullest.

Here's how I'm going to achieve it.

I plan to achieve my 1:1 Passive Income Ratio by earning $_____ in passive income by _____.

I plan to achieve my 2:1 Passive Income Ratio by earning $_____ in passive income by _____.

I plan to achieve my 5:1 Passive Income Ratio and be completely financially independent by earning $_____ in passive income by _____.

I plan to achieve my 10:1 Passive Income Ratio and have a sustainable amount of financial wealth by earning $_____ in passive income by _____.

To review passive income ratios, go to chapter 4.

Signature: _____

Date: _____

Go to our website to download and print this worksheet at 5DayWeekend.com.
Code: P16

5 Day Weekend Passport Resources

Go to our website for these free resources — 5DayWeekend.com

	Passport Resource	Book Page	Website Code
1	Passive Income Score Sheet	42	P1
2	Call to Action: Your 5 Day Weekend Plan	46	P2
3	Rockefeller Formula	83	P3
4	Call to Action: Your Debt Free Plan	89	P4
5	Income Opportunity Score Sheet	132	P5
6	The Idea Optimizer	133	P6
7	Call to Action: Your Entrepreneurial Income Plan	139	P7
8	Real Estate Cash Flow & ROI Calculator	164	P8
9	Tax Lien Investing	184	P9
10	The Sharelord Renting Strategy	186	P10
11	The Bank Strategy	188	P11
12	Cryptocurrencies	199	P12
13	Call to Action: Your Investing Plan	218	P13
14	Call to Action: Your Power Up! Plan	243	P14
15	Call to Action: Your Freedom Lifestyle Plan	281	P15
16	Call to Action: Your 5 Day Weekend Plan Contract	297	P16

ENDNOTES

1 https://www.conference-board.org/publications/publicationdetail.cfm ?publicationid=2785

2 www.weforum.org/agenda/2016/01/5-million-jobs-to-be-lost-by-2020/

3 https://www.ftc.gov/news-events/press-releases/2013/02/ftc-study -five-percent-consumers-had-errors-their-credit-reports

4 Note that this is a hypothetical example only. You need to be aware of all the rules before leveraging your Cash Flow Insurance policy to invest. For example, if you don't repay the loan during your lifetime, your death benefit will be reduced. Furthermore, if you don't do it right, you could lose your policy. Consult with a specialist first before setting up your policy.

5 Barry Dyke. *The Pirates of Manhattan* (Orlando, Fl. International Drive, 2007).

6 http://sethgodin.typepad.com/seths_blog/2014/12/where-to-start.html

7 https://en.wikipedia.org/wiki/Fiverr

8 http://www.go-globe.com/blog/mobile-apps-usage/

9 http://fortune.com/2015/07/29/video-game-coach-salary/

10 https://en.wikipedia.org/wiki/Sharing_economy

11 https://hbr.org/2015/01/the-sharing-economy-isnt-about-sharing -at-all

12 Cecilia Kang, "Podcasts Are Back—and Making Money," *Washington Post,* September 25, 2014. https://www.washingtonpost .com/business/technology/podcasts-are-back--and-making-money/ 2014/09/25/54abc628-39c9-11e4-9c9f-ebb47272e40e_story.html ?utm_term=.3bc42ee6f691

13 http://www.edisonresearch.com/wp-content/uploads/2016/05/ The-Podcast-Consumer-2016.pdf

14 http://www.globalwellnessinstitute.org/global-wellness-institute -study-34-trillion-global-wellness-market-is-now-three-times-larger -than-worldwide-pharmaceutical-industry/

15 http://www.statista.com/topics/962/global-tourism/

16 App.topica.com/banners/forms/900067555/.../SELLERSVSBUYER-SWHOWINS.doc

17 www.cbsnews.com/news/retirement-dreams-disappear-401ks/

18 Richard Paul Evans, The Five Lessons a Millionaire Taught Me About Life and Wealth (New York: Simon & Schuster, 2006).

19 www.nature.com/articles/nature04053

20 Maggie Fox, "Feeling Tired? Exercise a Little," Reuters, February 29, 2008. http://www.reuters.com/article/us-exercise-fatigue-idUSN2922162420080229

21 Lloyd Steven Sieden, *Buckminster Fuller's Universe: His Life and Work* (New York: Basic Books, 1989), pp. 87–88.

22 Phil Patton, "A 3-Wheel Dream That Died at Takeoff," *New York Times,* June 15, 2008.

23 Source: www.grameen.com

24 https://www.jstor.org/stable/2489522?seq=1#page_scan_tab_contents

25 https://www.sciencedaily.com/releases/2010/03/100322092057.htm

26 http://dare.uva.nl/cgi/arno/show.cgi?fid=609413

27 www.mindful.org/jon-Kabat-Zinn-zinn-defining-mindfulness/

28 www.newyorker.com/magazine/2003/10/13/jumpers

29 http://www.apa.org/research/action/rich.aspx

30 https://www.psychologytoday.com/blog/significant-results/201302/how-avoid-regret

31 https://www.huffingtonpost.com/2016/12/12/international-day-of-happiness-helping-_n_6905446.html

32 http://www.telegraph.co.uk/news/features/3634620/Miserable-Bored-You-must-be-rich.html

INDEX

ACKNOWLEDGMENTS

From Nik

As I reflect on the magnitude of this project, I think back on chapters that were written in exotic locations—sailing down the Nile River in Egypt, on a yacht in the Greek islands, or in a jet cruising at 40,000 feet.

I would dearly love to thank those who have played a significant role in my life—and in the making of this book.

First, my mother Dionisia, for believing in me and exhibiting incredible determination throughout my life. To Cintya, Victoria, Georgia, and Jim, for your unconditional love, support, commitment, and respect. You inspire me to dream big and live with passion.

To my dearest friend Bob Proctor, for your wisdom, dedication to the personal development field and for instilling in me the belief that we were all born rich.

To Ray Bard of Bard Press, thank you for your faith in me. Thank you for your inspirational guidance, dedication, passion, and unwavering commitment to this project. A great deal of gratitude, my friend.

To Garrett Gunderson, for sharing your valuable information, financial expertise, and aspiring story of economic freedom. Thank you for being a beacon of light on this project.

To my clients who have attended my Masterminds and Entrepreneurial training conferences, I acknowledge you for your active participation and massive action. For all my logistics staff assisting me with the running of our 5 Day Weekend events on five continents, thank you for your support in transforming lives.

To the giants whose shoulders I stand upon, the mentors who have shaped my life, philosophy, wisdom, and unwavering determination, I acknowledge and salute you.

Dare to dream. Live with Purpose. Make your life an epic, extraordinary adventure.

From Garrett

This has been an exciting and expanding project for me. Nik Halik, thanks for being a prime example of the 5 Day Weekend, leading me to an even better quality of life with our association.

To Ray Bard and the Bard Press team, your level of care, involvement, feedback, and knowledge was far beyond my expectation, and I had high expectations, knowing you were the best in the business.

Mick Hines, brother, for your dedication to this project, traveling everywhere on a moment's notice and being my cornerman.

To my Wealth Factory crew: Norm (best man to have in the foxhole), Mat, Tom, Stephen, Wade, Dale, Tim, Matthew, Boon, Garrick, Aaron, David, Brandon, Tricia (always looking out for me), Amanda, Demi, and Nordy. You make this all possible and profitable. Thanks for your research, results, and partnership.

Dan Sullivan and Babs Smith, you were the first to show me the value of time off. Rich Christiansen, for being part of my inner circle and trusted advisor. Ryan, Moe, and Derick, for being on my board of trustees and being instrumental in my life. Mike Isom, for being my trusted friend and travel companion.

Jon and Missy Butcher, you raised the bar for quality of life. John Vieceli, for your laugh, being the ultimate athlete of non-athletic quasi-sports, and doing top-notch design work.

Mom and Dad, for always being there, doing so much to instill a strong work ethic, compassion, and family values in me. I love you.

To my boys, Breck and Roman. This book has within it the keys to living an extraordinary life. As part of my legacy, I am excited to put this in your hands and heart. I love you.

To my wife Carrie, my love and greatest confidant. You see the best in me, remind me of when I am off track, keep me focused on what is most important, and make this life so much more fun.

From Nik and Garrett

Michael Drew, for bringing this project to life. He brought us all together, contributed ideas throughout, encouraged us with his constant enthusiasm, and crafted the marketing strategy.

Cindé Johnson, Michael's essential right-hand, with the book team since the beginning, making all the logistics work, and providing exceptional support all along the way.

Stephen Palmer, for all your great wordsmithing. For over delivering and going above and beyond.

Charlie Fusco, for amplifying our voice and the 5 Day Weekend spirit.

Joe Polish, Yanik Silver, Robert Hughes and Sophia Umanski, Jayson Gaignard, Hollis Carter, Michael Lovitch, Roy Williams (Wizard Academy), for your educational platforms, writings, Masterminds, and leadership.

The Bard Press team. Robert Todd editor, for your ideas, encouragement, and fine editing. Randy Miyake and Gary Hespenheide at Hespenheide Design, for the terrific text and cover design. Deborah Costenbader, for your superb work managing all the critical details. Sherry Todd, for getting us to the printer on time. And Joe Pruss, for his ongoing support.

Jason West, Chris Zaino, Pete Vargas, for being the example to so many. Patrick Gentempo and JJ Virgin, for being the premiere advocates of our work. And to all our 5 Day Weekend and Wealth Factory members that now live, or aspire to live, the 5 Day Weekend lifestyle. You are the pinnacle of our mission outreach to educate one million people to economic independence.

READERS

Content Consultants
(aka Potential Customers)

Listening to your customers is always a good idea. In the book world, the best way is to send people the draft manuscript. Ask them to think like a reader, be brutally frank, and offer their best ideas of how to make it a better book.

Three different times we sent the manuscript to readers. Every time they were very helpful. Their feedback from the first round dramatically changed our plan for the book. In other rounds, we made adjustments to address their needs, and to clarify and strengthen the book's message and its value.

They also rated and gave us feedback on the title and subtitle, as well as the jacket design.

The book you have would not have been nearly as good without their comments and recommendations.

Many thanks to all of the readers.

Danny Blitz
Ben and Joyce Frank
David Hathaway
Robyn R. Jackson
Daniel Kimbley
Brian Kurtz
Melissa Lombard

Brent Longhurst
Stephanie Melish
David Polis
Scott Provence
Troy Remelski
Cynthia Robbins
Todd Sattersten

GARRETT B. GUNDERSON

Garrett is a *New York Times* bestselling author, founder of an Inc. 500 financial firm, Chief Wealth Architect of the Wealth Factory, paid contributor for *Forbes,* and frequent keynote speaker.

His book, *Killing Sacred Cows: Overcoming the Financial Myths That Are Destroying Your Prosperity,* is a valuable guide for creating sustainable wealth while avoiding financial mistakes.

Raised in rural Utah, he comes from a fourth-generation coal-mining family. His great-grandfather came to the U.S. in 1913 to build a better life for his family. It changed Garrett's future and financial destiny, and is what makes him so passionate about helping entrepreneurs and small business owners build their own wealth.

With dual citizenship in the U.S. and Italy, Garrett now lives in Salt Lake City with his wife and two children.

NIK HALIK

Nik enjoys his 5 Day Weekend lifestyle.

He has traveled to 149 countries and participated in all kinds of extreme adventures.

He has dived to the wreck of the RMS *Titanic*, climbed some of the world's highest peaks, done a HALO skydive above Mt. Everest, climbed into an erupting volcano crater, and recently visited North Korea.

He was trained by the Russian Cosmonaut Training Academy and was a backup astronaut for the TMA 13 NASA/Russian mission to the International Space Station.

Nik earned his financial and personal freedom by investing in real estate, the financial markets, and founding several enterprises. He is an angel investor and strategic adviser for tech startups and a stakeholder in a number of businesses around the world. He is a frequent keynote speaker at conferences and Masterminds.

Nik resides in the Hollywood Hills, Los Angeles, and has private residences in South Beach Miami, Morocco, Australia, and the Greek Islands.

Take the Challenge!

Make Your 5 Day Weekend Happen

You're about to take a big step.

Make a life-changing move.

We're here to help.

Visit us at 5DayWeekend.com for more resources, discover what others in the 5 Day Weekend community are doing, keep up with Nik's adventures, and keep learning new investing strategies from Nik and Garrett.

5DayWeekend.com

COPYRIGHT

5 Day Weekend
Freedom to Make Your Life and Work Rich with Purpose
Nik Halik — Garrett Gunderson

Published by Bard Press, Austin, Texas

Ordering Information
For additional copies, contact your favorite bookstore or email info@bardpress.com.
Quantity discounts are available.

ISBN
13 digit: 978-1-885167-81-1

Publisher's Cataloging-In-Publication Data
Names: Halik, Nik. | Gunderson, Garrett B.
Title: 5 Day Weekend : freedom to make your life and work rich with purpose / Nik Halik
    [and] Garrett B. Gunderson.
Other Titles: 5Day Weekend
Description: First edition. | Austin, Texas : Bard Press, [2017] | "A Bard Press book." | Includes
    bibliographical references and index.
Identifiers: ISBN 9781885167811 | ISBN 1885167814
Subjects: LCSH: Finance, Personal. | Entrepreneurship. | Income. | Investments. | Liberty.
Classification: LCC HG179 .H35 2017 | DDC 332.024--dc23

A Bard Press book
Credits
Managing Editor: Sherry Todd
Substantive Editor: Robert Todd
Copyeditor/Production Editor: Deborah Costenbader
Proofreaders: Luke Torn, Raymond P. Urbina, and S. Gail Woods
Text Design and Illustrations: Hespenheide Design
Text Production: Hespenheide Design
Jacket Design: Hespenheide Design
Index: Roland Denney

First Edition
First printing: January 2018

CONTACT INFORMATION

Quantity Discounts Available

For additional copies of

5 Day Weekend

visit your favorite bookstore

or

email info@bardpress.com

5 DAY WEEKEND® MANIFESTO

I own my life. I set the terms. I take responsibility for my results. I am the master of my fate, the determiner of my destiny. I live by design, not by default.

I reject the grind of 9 to 5. I escape the oppression of time clocks and bosses, commuting and cubicles.

I do not yearn for security but hunger for freedom. I renounce the dependence of jobs and benefits, and create independence through entrepreneurship.

I build businesses for cash flow, while others slave at jobs for a salary.

I create wealth by investing in assets, while others create liabilities on credit.

I am willing to do what others will not do, to get what others will not enjoy.

I hustle for a short time to fully enjoy life for a long time.

5 DAY W